MARCO ⊕ POLO

Insider Tips

NAPLES &
THE AMALFI COAST

AUSTRIA
HUNGARY
SLOVENIA
Milan
CROATIA
ITALY
BOSNIA
&HERZEG.
RSM
SERBIA
Corsica
(F)
MNE RKS
Rome
MAC
Naples
ALBA-
Sardinia
NIA
(I)
Tyrrhenian
Sea
GREECE
Mediterranean
Sea
Sicily

SYMBOLS

INSIDER TIP	Insider Tip
★	Highlight
🔵🔵🔵⚫	Best of...
🗻	Scenic view
🌍	Responsible travel: for ecological or fair trade aspects
(*)	Telephone numbers that are not toll-free

PRICE CATEGORIES HOTELS

Expensive over 160 euros

Moderate 100–160 euros

Budget under 100 euros

Prices for a double room including breakfast in intermediate season

PRICE CATEGORIES RESTAURANTS

Expensive over 20 (15) euros

Moderate 10–20 (8–15) euros

Budget under 10 (8) euros

Prices for a main meal *(secondo)* or a pasta dish *(primo,* in brackets) without side dishes and without the charge for bread and place settings

CONTENTS

DID YOU KNOW?
Timeline → p. 14
Books & Films → p. 22
Slow Food in Campania
→ p. 25
Local specialities → p. 28
National holidays → p. 119
Currency converter → p. 123
Budgeting → p. 124
Weather → p. 125

MAPS IN THE GUIDEBOOK
(132 A1) Page numbers and
coordinates refer to the road
atlas
(U A1) Refers to the city map
of Naples inside the back
cover
(0) Site/address located off
the map
Coordinates are also given for
places that are not marked
on the road atlas
Map of Herculaneum → p. 50
Map of Pompeii → p. 54

(*A–B 2–3*) refers to the
removable pull-out map
(*a–b 2–3*) refers to the
set map on the pull-out

INSIDE FRONT COVER
The best Highlights

INSIDE BACK CO
Citymap of Na

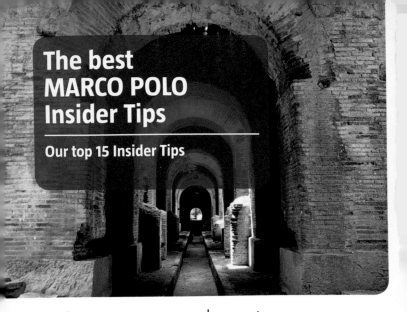

The best MARCO POLO Insider Tips

Our top 15 Insider Tips

INSIDER TIP **Red coral**

The *Museo del Corallo* is a real gem for jewellery lovers. Located in a secluded spot on the first floor of the Galleria Umberto I, the museum exhibits beautiful items of jewellery to trace back 200 years of coral jewellery manufacture → **p. 30**

INSIDER TIP **Leafy meeting place under the trees**

Stroll around the *Piazza Bellini* in Naples and absorb the atmosphere – it is always lively until late into the night with a variety of cafés including the literary café, Intra Moenia, the first women's bookstore in Naples, Caffè Arabo, and a vegetarian ethno restaurant → **p. 43**

INSIDER TIP **Explore the culinary side** ...mpania

...ck to the roots of Neapolitan ...y tasting the specialty *ragù* ...aised in tomato sauce) ...variety of ways at the ...estaurant → **p. 42**

INSIDER TIP **Baroque music at the source**

Celebrated on international stages, at home in Naples (and for visitors at really affordable prices!): the *Pietà de' Turchini* Ensemble → **p. 43**

INSIDER TIP **Colourfully illustrated biblical scenes**

The *medieval frescos* in the Basilica Sant'Angelo in Formis are beautifully preserved. Keep an eye out for the unusual square halo in the apse! → **p. 47**

INSIDER TIP **Ancient mothers**

Poignant, but rarely visited: the collection of votive statues from the Campanian fertility cult Mater Matuta in Capua → **p. 47**

INSIDER TIP **An oasis for the senses**

The *Negombo* thermal park in Ischia may no longer be a secret – but its excellent terrace restaurant still is → **p. 64**

BEST OF...

FOR FREE

● *Spas for free*
More than 100 thermal springs bubble forth on Ischia and thermal parks set in lush subtropical gardens guarantee spa and bathing pleasures. Enjoy the hot thermal waters in the sea at *Sorgeto Bay* entirely for free → p. 65

● *Musica napoletana*
Naples is music. Be it the sound of Homer's sirens, lyric villanelles that have been around since 16th century, "O sole mio", the blues by Pino Daniele, jazz à la James Senese or reggae rhythms by Almamegretta. Always and everywhere, thanks to the *Radio Partenope Web Radio* app → p. 121

● *Wacky art*
Internationally renowned artists and architects have designed the *Metro line 1 stations (Metrò dell'Arte)* in Naples, and sometimes even the nearby squares. Get art for free when you buy your Metro ticket! (photo) → p. 37

● *Oasis of calm*
In the Via San Gregorio Armeno lies the entrance to one of the most peaceful places in Naples' *centro storico*: the *garden in the San Gregorio Armeno cloister.* You need only ring the bell to be let in → p. 47

● *A view for millionaires*
Where the ancient Romans built their villas – overlooking the sea in Sorrento – today there are luxury hotels. You can enjoy the same (free) panorama from the *Villa Comunale public park* → p. 80

● *Art and coffee*
The renowned *Gran Caffè Gambrinus* is a coffee shop and art gallery rolled into one: the walls of the café are covered in pictures from the most famous Neapolitan artists from the late 19th century → p. 41

◖◖◗◗● Dots in guidebook refer to "Best of..." tips

● *Pizza Nazionale*

Real pizza, *la vera pizza*, is only available at its place of origin, right here in Napoli. For connoisseurs, only the original *Marinara* (tomatoes, garlic, oregano) and *Margherita* in the national colours (red, white, green: tomatoes, mozzarella, basil) count. It is expecially good at *Gino Sorbillo* → **p. 41**

● *Gelato al Limone*

This area is famed for its lemons and tempts with its Limoncello (photo), freshly squeezed lemonade *spremuta di limone* or the creamy *delizia al limone* dessert. Enjoy the refreshing and delicious *gelato al limone* in the *Buonocore* ice cream parlour in Capri! → **p. 61**

● *Endless views*

Panoramic views are always worth the effort. On the high hiking trail *Sentiero degli Dei* you are rewarded with magnificent views all the way from Capri to Cilento → **p. 71**

● *Heat beneath your feet*

The island of Ischia is one gigantic volcanic outcrop. You can literally feel the heat under your feet on the grey sand at the *Spiaggia dei Maronti* → **p. 63**

● *Tuff on tuff*

Naples is built on and from the rock known as tuff: Since antiquity, this volcanic rock has been excavated 40 m/131 ft underground and the quarried stone used to build houses. This excavation has created a labyrinth of tunnels and can be visited today at the unique *Napoli Sotterranea* museum → **p. 38**

● *Famed blood miracle and cult of saints*

Three times a year the patron saint of Naples, San Gennaro, liquefies his blood to the delight of his worshippers. However Saint Gennaro's blood is not the only one to liquefy, there are countless other saints who are worshipped in Naples → **p. 25, 36**

● *Pastry poetry*

Naples' most famous pastry is the *sfogliatella:* crisp puff pastry on the outside and inside a warm, fragrant ricotta flavoured with candied orange peel. Especially good at *Chalet Ciro* → **p. 41**

ONLY IN

BEST OF...

AND IF IT RAINS?
Activities to brighten your day

● **Naples' underground**
Discover the *catacombs:* Greek aqueducts, Roman neighbourhoods, early Christian frescos and the cult of the dead → **p. 36**

● **Stalactites and stalagmites**
There is a remarkable karst cave system in Cilento, the most impressive of which is the *Grotte di Castelcivita*, an extensive cave full of enchanting stalagmite and stalactite formations → **p. 93**

● **Naples on stage**
The most surprising thing about the ambitious *Napoli Teatro Festival Italia* is the selection of unusual venues (usually under a roof), such as the *Albergo dei Poveri* → **p. 118**

● **Sunshine, even when it rains**
The warm, friendly and bright interior and the delicious flavour of sun-ripened organic tomatoes, olives and lemons make for an unforgettable meal at the Michelin starred *Ristorante Don Alfonso 1890* in Sant'Agata sui Due Golfi → **p. 83**

● **Take the plunge**
When it rains, the ocean takes on wonderful colours and feels much warmer. Put on your mask, flippers and take the plunge (photo), for example in *Baia*. But when there is a thunderstorm it's better to be on dry land → **p. 113**

● **Bespoke brolly for a stroll through Naples**
If you are taken by surprise with rainy weather, you can continue your sightseeing tour with a dry head of hair with an umbrella made by *Talarico*. The family business has been making the finest *ombrelli* by hand since 1860 → **p. 43**

RAIN

RELAX AND CHILL OUT
Take it easy and spoil yourself

● *Capri sunset*

Enjoying the sunset from a deck chair: fantastic at the *Lido del Faro* in Anacapri. Even better with a longdrink in hand, leading to a romantic dinner (photo) → **p. 61**

● *Luxury resort from Nero's reign*

Ancient Baia was the most luxurious spa resort in Roman times. Now 2000 years after Emperor Nero, you can still bask in the ancient Roman steam grottos at the thermal baths *Stufe di Nerone* → **p. 46**

● *In an open-top bus along Naples' gulf coast*

These double-decker buses are the perfect way to explore Naples' beauty and offer respite from walking along the city's pavements. The top-deck view over the villa district of Posillipo is priceless → **p. 123**

● *Dolce far niente in Positano*

A postcard idyll from the 1950s: take a shuttle boat from Positano out to the relaxing *beach bar Bagni d'Arienzo* with its clean and delightful black pebble beach → **p. 76**

● *Sauna like the ancient Romans*

The thermal springs of the Phlegraean Fields were fashionable back in Ancient Rome: the steam grottos of the *Terme di Agnano* promise relaxation and have healing powers → **p. 43**

● *View into the blue yonder*

The best thing about Villa Cimbrone in Ravello is the balcony viewpoint of the *Terrazza dell'Infinito.* The view over the infinite sea is balm for the soul → **p. 77**

● *Herb garden*

The re-created medieval medicinal herb garden, the *Giardini di Minerva* in Salerno is a beautiful oasis of calm. Herbal teas and refreshing lemonades are served on the terrace → **p. 75**

INTRODUCTION

DISCOVER THE GULF OF NAPLES!

No matter where you begin your Gulf of Naples journey – the most beautiful introduction has to be a *view over the Gulf*: for example from the Sorrento Peninsula, from the balconies and terraces of the gorgeous old hotels that rise high above the sea on the volcanic plateau of Sorrento. From here you can see across the entire arc of the Gulf, inland to the Monti Lattari mountain range, then on to the mighty *volcanic cone of Vesuvius*, and finally to the dense sea of roofs that make up the fascinating metropolis of Naples. Through the sea mist you can make out the islands of Ischia and Procida, Capri on the other hand is hidden by the tip of the Sorrento Peninsula. Islands of promise – and each with its own unique character.

Beyond the Sorrento Peninsula lies Amalfi's *Costa Divina* (divine coast) with its lemon grove terraces, charming villages that cling precariously to the mountainsides, nestled with pastel coloured houses and overgrown with *bright red bougainvillea vines*. This marvellous coast has held generations of visitors under its spell and they return again and again to wander along the old trade paths high above the Costiera Amalfitana, revelling in the atmosphere. This is also where you'll find some of the most beautiful hotels – hospitality is an age-old tradition on the Amalfitana. In the 19th century

The gorge in the Calore River beyond Cilento shows a different side of Campania

medieval monasteries and aristocratic palaces were converted into luxury hotels and today the range of accommodation includes *charming B&Bs* in secluded vineyards or picturesque old fishing houses.

Some of the finest dining can be had on the Sorrento Peninsula where numerous high-profile gourmet restaurants have recently opened. They draw in even the most demanding customers with their creative, but entirely traditional, Campania cuisine. There is ample evidence that the garden gods took a special liking to this region, especially when you see the markets in the towns and villages along the coastal road: *mounds of citrus fruits*, fresh artichokes, sweet sun-ripened tomatoes, crisp vegetables, apricots, pears, grapes, loquats, figs, and all of it juicy and freshly picked.

8th–5th century BC
Along the coast, and on Ischia, Greek colonies develop, one of which was the "new town" Neapolis

From 4th/3rd century BC
Romanisation of Greek cities, the Roman upper class built superbly situated villas

AD 79
An eruption of Mount Vesuvius buries the Roman cities of Herculaneum, Pompeii and Stabiae under lava and ash

11th–13th century
Under the rule of the Normans and the Hohenstaufen dynasty, southern Italy forms a political unity

The Amalfi Coast opens on to the Gulf of Salerno where the ancient port city of Salerno has recently blossomed – star architects such as Zaha Hadid, Oriol Bohigas and Santiago Calatrava have made their mark – and it is also a prelude to the *Cilento* region. This region in Campania's very south is a positive example of the interaction between a protected cultural (and natural) landscape and environmentally friendly tourist developments.

It begins with Paestum, the wonderfully preserved, *ancient temples* on the plain of the Sele River, and then rises to massive mountain ranges with peaks up to almost 1900 m/6233 ft high. Here you can discover an old farming countryside, a coastline of fantastic rock formations and magical sandy dunes. Inland you can hike in *protected forests*, visit mysterious caves or spend some time on an *agriturismo* farm. On the coast there are camp sites in olive groves and holiday resorts on pristine beaches with crystal-clear sea. Just the right contrast to the hustle and bustle of Naples.

Rocky coast and bays, forests and grottos

Naples is an Italian city that polarises like no other – the refuse removal scandal, the bloody feuds of the Camorra and various environmental catastrophes spring immediately to mind. Fortunately, the *political and cultural upswing* has not taken a knock. Everyone is speaking of the new underground with its stations designed by avantgarde artists. Everywhere visitors are impressed by carefully restored *palazzi* and

1647/48 A tax on fresh fruit creates a popular uprising, under the leadership of fishmonger Tommaso Aniello ("Masaniello"), against the rule of Habsburg Spain

1734 Bourbon King Charles III conquers Naples. The excavations in Pompeii begin

1860 Naples votes to join the newly developed national state of Italy

1943 The *Quattro Giornate di Napoli*, a popular uprising in which the locals force out the fascists and Nazis occupiers

Fullness of life and soul in a magnificent setting

churches as well as small private museums and cultural initiatives – together they transform the centre of the Old Town into a *lively cultural conglomerate.*

People like to meet in this historical setting: on the Piazza Bellini (in the evenings, a younger crowd) and (especially on Sundays) on the wide Piazza del Plebiscito in front of the Palazzo Reale. At one point a chaotic car park, now an outdoor stage and concert arena, a popular backdrop for wedding photographers, strolling Neapolitans and tourists as well as a playground for lively children. The *centro storico*, the most densely populated old town in Europe, still belongs to its residents and not just the banks and chic offices. Even its listing as a Unesco World Heritage Site in 1995 has not changed the historic centre. Naples is a *vibrant city and not a museum* but this also means that there are narrow alleys, run-down urban "canyons" in areas such as the Quartieri Spagnoli or Sanità with dark basement flats *(bassi)* and everywhere small altars dot the streets and courtyards – no idyll but certainly a life with lots of heart that is lived in a magnificent setting.

Today exhibitions and concerts flourish, the large Neapolitan museums such as the Palace of Capodimonte with its famous art collection, the Archaeological Museum

Tunnels dating back to the Greeks and Romans

with the *treasures from Pompeii*, the lovely city museum with the Neapolitan nativity scenes in the Carthusian monastery of San Martino – they have all been restored and now attract tourists in their

droves. With museums such as the MADRE and PAN and the private Museo Hermann Nitsch, *contemporary art* has also been able to find its place in the Gulf of Naples. And a group of amateur speleologists have explored Naples' underworld – cisterns, caves, tunnels in the volcanic rock that date back to the Greeks, Romans and Bourbons, a breathtaking counter world to the bright city above.

The Neapolitans love their city – you will often meet locals who make it their concern to show tourists a hidden treasure, a chapel, an extraordinarily beautiful courtyard – often with warm, polite friendliness. This proud courtesy dates back to a *highly cultural past*, to the ancient Greeks, whose impressive traces you will encounter every-

1950s Beginning of the destructive construction boom in Naples

1980 Heavy earthquake in Campania

2007 Bloody feuds within the Camorra, waste removal problems and tighter security measures make life in Naples challenging

2015 The centre-left party of Minister President Vincenzo de Luca wins the local elections. Inauguration of the underground metro station, Municipio, the last station in the line of spectacular art stations on the Neapolitan metro

where on your trip through Campania, as well as to a time when Naples was the capital of a kingdom for centuries, with a magnificent court and everything that belongs with it.

The settlement on the southern Italian coast began in 770 BC when exiled Greeks, who first landed on Ischia, founded the Pithekussai colony. Some 45 years later they moved to Cuma on the mainland and founded settlements in the Naples area. In Campania's hinterland the Etruscans and Apennine tribes settled here first, later the Romans entered the fray. They were enchanted by the beauty of the Gulf, Campania's coast and the islands and fascinated by the Greek-influenced life in Naples: everywhere, thermal baths and beautiful, *historic villas* built around them sprang up. With the fall of the Roman Empire, new people and foreign ruling dynasties advanced to the south. In 1137 the Normans took over Naples and with them came the establishment of a feudal centralized administration in the south of Italy – initially under the Anjou, then under the house of Aragón, and finally under the Bourbons until the creation of the national state of Italy in 1861. Some of the traces of this impressive historical legacy are now world-class sightseeing attractions, but also *nature and national parks* and vibrant cities – all waiting to be explored and enjoyed.

Naples' problems – unemployment, organised crime, relentless urban sprawl, pollution, traffic chaos – are all still part and parcel of the city. But those who travel to the Gulf of Naples are usually looking for *real life, with all its contradictions*, and do not just want to lie in their deckchairs.

Amalfi landmark: Piazza del Duomo with steps leading up to the cathedral

WHAT'S HOT

1 Chilometro zero

Regional cuisine Even the Gulf of Naples is slowly but surely developing an environmental awareness. The *chilometro zero (0 km)* or "zero food miles" movement is a clear indication of this trend which promotes locally grown food, mainly fruit and vegetables. The short food supply chain not only preserves freshness and quality but also saves on energy. Francesco Civita and his young team at *Eatinitaly (www.eatinitalyfoodtours.com)* exclusively use zero food mile ingredients for their pizza baking course in Naples. They also organise tours to trattorias that promote the zero food mile philosophy.

Swim-trekking

2

Water adventure Neither on foot nor by boat – instead visitors explore the region by swimming in the coves and grottos of Praiano. There is even a wonderful cave concert *(www.isuonideglidei.com)* held in one of the stunning grottos. Swimmers are led by professionals from *ASD Swimtrekking (www.swimtrekking.com)*.

3 Back to nature

Ice age Organic ingredients, eco-packaging and a social commitment: if it weren't for the calories, you could enjoy the ice cream from ☻ *Bianco Bio (Via Enrico Alvino 13)* in Naples without a guilty conscience. The *Gelateria Matteo (Via del Centenario 130)* in Lancusi roasts its own hazelnuts, before they are processed further into *gelato di nocciole.* The walnuts used by *Gelateria Davide (Via Marziale 19)* near the station in Sorrento are also from local producers.

Let the music play on

Live & loud There is no shortage of arenas and concert halls on the Gulf of Naples. But it is not only classical music that has found its place here, also pop and rock music. You'll find mostly local bands performing at *Mamamu (Via Sedile di Porto 46 | www.mamamu.altervista.org)* in Naples and when they do the place gets really packed, the balcony is the ideal spot from which to watch the acts. On Sundays they show avant-garde films. The tiny yet lively jazz club *Bourbon Street (Via Vincenzo Bellini 52 | www.bourbonstreetjazzclub.com)* attracts crowds on Friday evenings with its live concerts. There is also the *Galleria Toledo (Via Concezione a Montecalvario 34)* theatre in Naples that shows art house films in summer while in winter live music becomes the main focus. Those looking to dance the night away should head to *La Mela (Via dei Mille 41 | www.lamelaclub.it)* which maintains its reputation as the city's coolest disco.

4

The art world

5

Informal Art galleries should not deter but invite you to enjoy. The *Trip (Via Martucci 64 | www.tripnapoli.com | photo)* in Naples wants to break down all the barriers to art – its relaxed bar and garden lessens the intimidation of the creative scene for art newbies. It is as relaxed at the *Galleria Umberto Di Marino (Via Alabardieri 1|, www.galleriaumbertodimarino.com)*. Re-inventing plastic: the interactive museum *Fondazione Plart (Via Martucci 48 | www.fondazioneplart.it)* leads you through the world of plastic design and art.

IN A NUTSHELL

CAFFÈ

Many believe that the word *espresso* – a small cup of strong coffee – is typically Italian but the Italians actually say *caffè*. They drink it at the counters of the many standing bars found on the street corners and squares and its fragrance is often stronger than that of the city's exhaust fumes. Italian coffee is considered one of the best in the world but in Naples *caffè* has reached perfection: full bodied yet smooth, strong yet aromatic and neither bitter nor acidic. It has less to do with good quality coffee beans and more to do with the skill of the *barista* who operates the espresso machine. It is their task to adjust the grind of the bean, to prepare the grounds and to then apply just the right amount of pressure for the ideal amount of steam to produce the perfect cup. Neapolitans also believe that the quality of their coffee has something to do with the quality of their water. In summer coffee is also served cold as *caffè freddo* or semi-frozen as *granita*. Unique to Naples is the old tradition – *caffè sospeso* (coffee in suspension) where a customer orders one *caffè* but pays for two. This means that a person who is down on their luck can come in and enjoy a coffee courtesy of a kind benefactor – a human right in Naples.

CAMORRA

If you buy brand knock-offs from the street markets in Naples then you will also be supporting the Camorra and organised crime. Apart from pirated products, their

2015 and mixed jazz, blues a
melodies with English and Nea
lyrics in a unique blend that is po
over Italy, while the band Alma
mixes old *tammurriata* rhythms w
and reggae and Neapolitan dialec
There is also the so-called *neom*
where the lyrics are in the Neapolitan
and the sound is a mix of electron
and folk music. The musicians are
larly popular with the urban workin
where they are celebrated as local pop
and they don't shy away from the Car
The old pop singer and ex-prime mi
Silvio Berlusconi has had less success
his Neapolitan love songs: he releas
CD done in collaboration with the si
(ex-parking attendant and entertaine
Berlusconi's infamous parties) Mari
Apicella but the CD hasn't sold well.

LOTTERY

The Neapolitans all seem to believe
the power of fate and are fanatical lotte
players. Figuring out how best to pred

Camorra, saints and the lottery – interesting facts about pizza, "O sole mio" and other typical Neapolitan phenomena

big business, where they make vast sums of money, consists of drugs, weapons, waste management as well as extortion and blackmail – and, of course, construction. The organisation is made up of family clans which operate independently of one another. Over the last 20 years, the Camorra has been held responsible for 335 murders in Naples and the Campania region. Besides the large number of victims, the leniency programme has also led to successful arrests of clan members. But as long as more than half of the

460,000 unemployed in Campania are the youth, who see little chance of opportunities for themselves in the normal way, the Camorra will continue to have new adherents.

Alongside government efforts to fight organised crime, the 🌐 anti mafia organisation *Libera (www.libera.it)* has also been active since 1995. It runs a store called 🌐 *Bottega dei Sapori e dei Saperi* ("shop of good taste and good conscience") in the Via Raffaele de Cesare 28 in Naples where it sells products grown

by cooperatives on Camor[...]
which has been seized by [...]
tins of tomatoes, pasta, oliv[...]
all organically grown produ[...]

CANZONE NAPO[...]

Naples is a musical city [...]
metropolis of melodrama in [...]
tury – and it has spawned fam[...]
musicians, composers and [...]
melodic songs (that are alm[...]
know as the Bible!) such as "[...]
"Funiculì Funiculà", "Santa Luc[...]
a Surriento", "Marechiaro" [...]

BOOKS & FIL[...]

Pompeii – Robert Harris has p[...]
duced an accurately researche[...]
torical novel that has proven a[...]
success. Exciting and highly inf[...]
tive, this is the story of the app[...]
ing catastrophe and eruption o[...]
Vesuvius in AD 79

For Grace Received – this is a coll[...]
of novellas by Valeria Parella (a y[...]
feminist writer who is a strong Gu[...]
of Naples literary voice) who vivid[...]
connects the city's modern inhabit[...]
with its complex past

Dreaming by Numbers – written a[...]
directed by Anna Bucchetti (2003) [...]
film is a respectful portrayal of the [...]
poor and disadvantaged of Naples, [...]
who try to make it in this world with[...]
the help of a complicated lottery nu[...]
ber system

The Postman (Il Postino) – the [...]
island of Procida provides the back-[...]
drop for the poetic friendship be-

FOOD & DRINK

There is hardly any other region in Italy that is as lush and as fruitful as Campania. On the outskirts of Naples the green *campania felix* (the "happy country") spreads out.

Here lie the carefully cultivated fields with dark, rich volcanic soil, where **countless varieties of fruit and vegetables** grow year round: artichokes, broccoli, *cime de rapa* (a kale variety), the typically Campanian *friarielli* (a slightly peppery leaf vegetable), young green asparagus, peppers, aubergines, zucchini and every type of salad leaf and cabbage.

Everywhere there are **tomatoes**: the large, bright red meaty tomatoes from Sorrento, ideal as a salad and in the *caprese*, then the small, sweet cherry tomatoes, the *pomodorini del piennolo*, which thrive in the fertile soil around Mount Vesuvius, and are sun-dried in bundles then used as a pizza base, on *bruschetta* and in to-mato stock. The most famous tomatoes from the *campania felix* are, however, the heirloom variety of plum tomato or the *pummarola*, as the Neapolitans say, the *San Marzano,* from which the *sugo* is prepared. *Sugo* is added to spaghetti and macaroni, *bucatini, fusilli, vermicelli, sci-alatelli, cavatelli* all the **kinds of pasta**. The *sugo* sauce is also used to cook fish and meat in, and you simply can't have a pizza without the tomato sauce as its base. Olives, capers, oregano, garlic, *pep-eroncino* (chilli), and basil are the season-ings.

In addition to the tomatoes, the pasta also plays a crucial role. The traditional local

Bild: *spaghetti alle vongole*

Camorra, saints and the lottery – interesting facts about pizza, "O sole mio" and other typical Neapolitan phenomena

big business, where they make vast sums of money, consists of drugs, weapons, waste management as well as extortion and blackmail – and, of course, construction. The organisation is made up of family clans which operate independently of one another. Over the last 20 years, the Camorra has been held responsible for 335 murders in Naples and the Campania region. Besides the large number of victims, the leniency programme has also led to successful arrests of clan members. But as long as more than half of the 460,000 unemployed in Campania are the youth, who see little chance of opportunities for themselves in the normal way, the Camorra will continue to have new adherents.

Alongside government efforts to fight organised crime, the 🌎 anti mafia organisation *Libera (www.libera.it)* has also been active since 1995. It runs a store called 🌎 *Bottega dei Sapori e dei Saperi* ("shop of good taste and good conscience") in the Via Raffaele de Cesare 28 in Naples where it sells products grown by cooperatives on Camorra estate land which has been seized by the state, e.g. tins of tomatoes, pasta, olive oil and wine, all organically grown products.

CANZONE NAPOLETANA

Naples is a musical city – it was the metropolis of melodrama in the 18th century – and it has spawned famous singers, musicians, composers and wonderfully melodic songs (that are almost as well know as the Bible!) such as "O sole mio", "Funiculì Funiculà", "Santa Lucia", "Torna a Surriento", "Marechiaro" and many more. The *canzone napoletana* are sung in the local dialect and celebrate Neapolitan life. A good (not too sentimental) exponent is Roberto Murolo. Today the city's vibrant musical heritage continues and in addition to the usual commercial folk music there are now some more unusual sounds: the famous Nuova Compagnia del Canto Popolare promote and revive old folk music and vocalists such as Edoardo Bennato and Teresa de Sio or the group Spaccanapoli, fuse Neapolitan folk with modern rhythms. A modern classic is Pino Daniele, who died in

BOOKS & FILMS

Pompeii – Robert Harris has produced an accurately researched historical novel that has proven a great success. Exciting and highly informative, this is the story of the approaching catastrophe and eruption of Vesuvius in AD 79

For Grace Received – this is a collection of novellas by Valeria Parella (a young feminist writer who is a strong Gulf of Naples literary voice) who vividly connects the city's modern inhabitants with its complex past

Dreaming by Numbers – written and directed by Anna Bucchetti (2003) this film is a respectful portrayal of the poor and disadvantaged of Naples, who try to make it in this world with the help of a complicated lottery number system

The Postman (Il Postino) – the island of Procida provides the backdrop for the poetic friendship between the exiled Chilean poet, Pablo Neruda, and the island's postman, played by the Massimo Troisi in this 1994 film

Gomorrah – in an explosive mixture of reportage and novel, journalist Roberto Saviano gives his insights into the economic network of the Camorra. The film, based on the bestseller, won the Cannes Grand Prix award in 2008

It Started in Naples – in this charming comedy (1960) American seriousness (Clark Gable) meets Italian joie de vivre (Sophia Loren) with magnificent Capri as the backdrop

The Talented Mr. Ripley – this psychological thriller (1999) takes place in Italy with some scenes shot in and around the sultry coast of Naples. It has a star-studded cast that includes Jude Law, Matt Damon, Gwyneth Paltrow and Cate Blanchett

Myths and miracles: saints are omnipresent in Naples

2015 and mixed jazz, blues and pop melodies with English and Neapolitan lyrics in a unique blend that is popular all over Italy, while the band Almamegretta mixes old *tammurriatu* rhythms with dub and reggae and Neapolitan dialect lyrics. There is also the so-called *neomelodici* where the lyrics are in the Neapolitan dialect and the sound is a mix of electronic, rap and folk music. The musicians are particularly popular with the urban working class where they are celebrated as local pop stars and they don't shy away from the Camorra. The old pop singer and ex-prime minister Silvio Berlusconi has had less success with his Neapolitan love songs: he released a CD done in collaboration with the singer (ex-parking attendant and entertainer at Berlusconi's infamous parties) Mariano Apicella but the CD hasn't sold well.

LOTTERY

The Neapolitans all seem to believe in the power of fate and are fanatical lottery players. Figuring out how best to predict the winning numbers has produced a veritable industry of numbers oracles and advisers, as well as "counsellors" who interpret dreams, events and experiences and then convert them into numbers. These lists of numbers are called *smorfie*, a term that comes from Morpheus, the god of sleep and dreams. In the historic old town area of Naples the lottery offices and bookmakers have plenty of *smorfie* books, a very Neapolitan curiosity. There documentary "Dreaming by Numbers" offers some fascinating insights into this elaborate system of choosing lottery numbers.

NATIVITY SCENES

In Naples Christmas decorations, in the form of nativity scenes, are everwhere and go beyond the usual manger scene to contemporary or humorous scenes with card playing or fish and vegetables vendors. Children and dogs scuffle and you find camels, chickens, and even lizards. All of this takes place in front of a backdrop of houses, ancient ruins, cliffs under a blue

The simple classic is best: the green, red and white Margherita

sky with clouds and beautiful angels. You have to really hunt around to find what the occasion is actually about: Mary, Joseph and baby Jesus in the manger. This miniature art form really exploded under the Bourbon King Charles III, when each church and each family, wanted their own nativity scene and what was intended as a pious undertaking on the theme of Christ's birth grew instead into "a collective madness" (Dario Cecchi). Hundreds of artisans worked throughout the year making figures and parts for the scenes, some were responsible for the vegetables, others for the animals. Great artists such as Giuseppe Sammartino and Domenico

Vaccaro created wonderful figures. You can admire some of their creations in the San Martino Museum. Actually, the nativity art can be seen as a visual expression of the love of live that characterises Neapolitans and the best place to find the widest selection of nativity pieces is in the Via San Gregorio Armeno, where it is Christmas all year round.

PIZZA

According to the Neapolitan novelist Domenico Rea, a pizza has to be "as round as the Gulf of Naples and so thin that the centre is almost transparent and the edge rises just like the coastline". But that is easier said than done. In addition to generations of experience, Naples' pizza bakers also have the best, fresh local ingredients at their disposal: sweet, sun-ripened San Marzano tomatoes and creamy buffalo mozzarella or *fior di latte* (from cow's milk) for the *pizza Margherita*, plump anchovies for *pizza Napoletana* and fragrant oregano for *pizza Marinara*. The traditional guild, the "Associazione Verace Pizza Napoletana" swears that these three pizzas are the only true pizzas. In Naples, pizza is celebrated every year at the end of September with a large festival *(www.pizzafestival.pizzanapoletana.org)*. The flat, round bread, seasoned with olive oil and oregano, first appeared on the streets of Naples in the 19th century as a cheap quick bite to eat. In 1895 Italian immigrants opened up the first pizzeria in America and today the pizza (along with the hamburger) is *the* snack worldwide. Despite globalisation: pizza still tastes best in Naples.

SAINTS

As you take your first walk through Naples you will immediately notice that every street corner and in almost every alley there is an illuminated wall shrine with a Madonna statue or saint behind glass or bars, lit by small lamps and decorated with artificial and fresh flowers. The poorer the area, the more lovingly maintained the shrines and their festive lights are often in stark contrast to the peeling and smog-grimed walls surrounding them. In Naples they pay homage to 52 different saints, seven of which are principle saints, and at the top is ● San Gennaro, the patron saint of Naples. Thrice a year the faithful gather to witness the liquefaction of a sample of his blood in an ampoule which takes place after fervent prayer. Belief is intertwined with everyday suvival where people feel at the mercy of others and seek protection from chaos and disorder; the high number of shrines is evidence of religious beliefs that are a blend of myth and legend harking back to the heritage of the hea-

then gods of the ancient Greeks and the Romans.

WASTE MANAGEMENT

Naples has acquired the dubious reputation of being Europe's "rubbish capital". Waste and its removal is a profitable business for the Camorra and waste is also a very political issue. According to Legambiente (the Italian environmental organisation), the Camorra clans turned a 20 billion euros profit in 2009 alone through waste removal, about ten times as much as, for example, the Benetton fashion group. The city's mayor, Luigi De Magistris, has launched the waste separation programme and called for a show of civil courage in the fight against the "waste mafia". However the problem is not the waste produced by locals but rather the fact that the Camorra has dumped toxic waste from Italy's North into Naples' landfills and continues to do so.

SLOW FOOD IN CAMPANIA

The internationally active Slow Food movement was founded in Italy in 1986 and is especially evident in Campania. The movement strives to preserve and promote traditional regional cuisine using local foods that are characteristic of the local ecosystem, produced by local businesses. Biodiversity, diversity of culinary cultures, fair conditions for producers and the enjoyment of the consumer are the movement's focus. Campania Slow Food products that include *alici di menaica,* anchovies that are caught using ancient methods by the fishermen in Pisciotta and preserved in brine. White artichokes from Pertosa, beans from Controne, the

Piennolo del Vesuvio tomato variety or the famous Pomodoro San Marzano (the best tinned tomatoes) are all taste ambassadors of the movement. The slow-food pope from Campania, Luciano Pignataro, posts restaurant tips on his blog *www. lucianopignataro.it.* Many restaurants mentioned in this travel guide – where you will also often meet interesting people – follow the Slow Food philosophy. The Slow Food movement inspired the *città slow* movement, a philosophy of sustainability and improved quality of life in towns. In Campania it includes towns such as Amalfi, Pollica and Positano. *www.slowfood.it/campania*

FOOD & DRINK

There is hardly any other region in Italy that is as lush and as fruitful as Campania. On the outskirts of Naples the green *campania felix* (the "happy country") spreads out.

Here lie the carefully cultivated fields with dark, rich volcanic soil, where **countless varieties of fruit and vegetables** grow year round: artichokes, broccoli, *cime de rapa* (a kale variety), the typically Campanian *friarielli* (a slightly peppery leaf vegetable), young green asparagus, peppers, aubergines, zucchini and every type of salad leaf and cabbage.

Everywhere there are **tomatoes**: the large, bright red meaty tomatoes from Sorrento, ideal as a salad and in the *caprese*, then the small, sweet cherry tomatoes, the *pomodorini del piennolo*, which thrive in

the fertile soil around Mount Vesuvius, and are sun-dried in bundles then used as a pizza base, on *bruschetta* and in tomato stock. The most famous tomatoes from the *campania felix* are, however, the heirloom variety of plum tomato or the *pummarola*, as the Neapolitans say, the *San Marzano,* from which the *sugo* is prepared. *Sugo* is added to spaghetti and macaroni, *bucatini, fusilli, vermicelli, scialatelli, cavatelli* all the **kinds of pasta**. The *sugo* sauce is also used to cook fish and meat in, and you simply can't have a pizza without the tomato sauce as its base. Olives, capers, oregano, garlic, *peperoncino* (chilli), and basil are the seasonings.

In addition to the tomatoes, the pasta also plays a crucial role. The traditional local

Finger food *alla napoletana* – fruit and vegetables thrive throughout the year in the fertile volcanic soil

kinds include *maccheroni della zita* (thick, long spaghetti), the thick and long *scialatielli,* often made by hand, and the short, broad tube noodles called *paccheri.* Campania also has many **seafood** and fish dishes including anchovies *(alici),* red mullet *(triglia),* scorpion fish *(scorfano),* red bream *(cernia),* sea bass *(dorata),* sole *(sogliola),* swordfish *(pesce spada),* mackerel *(sgombro),* squid *(calamaro, seppia),* octopus *(polipo),* but especially mussels *(cozze)* and the favourite **clams** *(vongole veraci).* A real Slow Food delicacy are the

INSIDER TIP anchovies from Cetara, on the Amalfi Coast *(alici cetaresi),* and from Pisciotta on the coast of Cilento.

Besides pork *(maiale)* and beef *(manzo),* **kid goat** *(capretto)* is a popular dish in Cilento while lamb *(agnello)* and rabbit *(coniglio)* are popular on Ischia. Buffalo meat is also growing in popularity. Vegetables are **marinated in oil**, stuffed, grilled, seasoned with lemon juice, garlic and *peperoncino*. But pasta is also often prepared with vegetables in all possible variations.

LOCAL SPECIALITIES

alici marinate – raw anchovies, marinated in lemon juice or vinegar, as a starter

all'acqua pazza – "in crazy water", fish in tomato sauce

alla pizzaiola – meat in tomato sauce with garlic and oregano

babà – small yeast cake, soaked in rum

calzone – pastry turn over from pizza dough, filled with ham, mozzarella, ricotta and parmesan

caponata – summer dish made with bread, tomatoes, olives, capers, oregano and oil

caprese – Italy's famous summer dish: mozzarella, tomatoes, basil (photo right)

gattò di patate – savoury bake made with potatoes, egg, ham or salami and cheese

impepata di cozze – mussels with lemon, parsley and freshly ground black pepper

mozzarella in carozza – crumbed, fried sandwiches, filled with mozzarella

parmigiana di melanzane – slices of aubergines, tomatoes, mozzarella, sprinkled with parmesan and baked in the oven

pastiera – a traditional Neapolitan Easter tart made with ricotta, cooked wheat, candied fruit, eggs and spices (photo left)

polipi affogati – small octopus, "drowned" in tomato stock

sfogliatelle – puff pastry filled with a mix of ricotta, candied fruit, vanilla and cinnamon

spaghetti alle vongole – spaghetti with small clams, garlic, and parsley

totani e patate – squid and potato stew

zucchine a scapece – fried zucchini slices, cooled with a dash of vinegar and mint

Sweets, pastries and desserts also have a long tradition in Campania and you will be spoilt for choice in every *pasticceria*, and even aubergines are coated with chocolate sauce here, and sometimes served as a dessert. Important ingredients are candied fruits and *ricotta*, the light fresh cheese made from cow or sheep milk whey. And then there are also some excellent cheeses in Campania. The king of the local cheeses has to be the buffalo milk *mozzarella (di bufala)*, light, moist and creamy – nothing at all like the rubbery mozzarella in our supermarkets. Other fresh cheeses are *scamorza*, which you can have either smoked or grilled, and the light yellow *provolone*, with is often used for *pizza calzone*. And they all go perfectly with the delicious and wholesome country loaf. For those small snacks in between meals you can also pop into a *rosticceria* or *tavola calda* snack bar for some *roba mischiata*: *finger foods* alla napoletana.

Naturally Campania also produces its own wines, and has done so for 3000 years. The vines on the slopes of Mount Vesuvius produce both red and white wines, which carry the *Lacryma Christi* (Christ's tears) label. **Excellent Campania white wines** are *Fiano di Avellino* and *Greco di Tufo* or the *Bianco d'Ischia*. While the fresh *Fiano* is best suited to fish and seafood, the fruity, often slightly sparkling *Greco di Tufo* is ideal as an aperitif.

Full-bodied Campania red wines are *Taurasi* and *Falerno* (the latter is also available as a white wine). The lightly sparkling *Gragnano* may be rather unpretentious, but it is just as good. Even though wines from Irpinia, which is how the Avellino province is also called, have been in the Italian top league for years, now the wines from Cilento have also stepped up to the plate in the annual "Vini d'Italia" wine tastings. This is thanks to the **dedication of vintners** such as Bruno De Conciliis, Luigi Maffini, Francesco Barone and newcomers Mario Corrado and Ida Budetta. They grow characteristic **indigenous varieties** such as *Aglianico* (red) and *Fiano* (white).

Regional **liqueurs** are *limoncello* or *limoncino* made from lemons, to be more precise: from the particularly thick skins

Whether restaurant or pizzeria: you can almost always sit outside in the south

of the typical Amalfi lemon, called *limone sfusato*. There is also *Amaro Strega* a herbal liqueur made in Benevento; the **walnuts** from the local groves are its main ingredient. And the perfect finale for every meal is, of course, a *caffè*.

SHOPPING

Traditional and modern arts and crafts, clothing, culinary treats, fine jewellery, chic fashions, second-hand and even stolen goods: the Gulf of Naples is a veritable treasure trove for the shopper.

CULINARY

At the start of the Sorrento Peninsula is Gragnano, a town that overlooks the Gulf of Naples, and one that is famous throughout Italy for its excellent INSIDER TIP durum wheat pasta. You can buy the pasta at grocery stores and in the local supermarkets. Among the culinary treats that make good souvenirs are also vegetables marinated in oil or vinegar – aubergines, zucchini, mushrooms, artichokes – the *sott'oli* or *sott'aceti*. Other options include the excellent extra-virgin olive oil from Cilento and of course the ever-present *limoncello*, the delicious lemon liqueur., especially from Capri, Sorrento and Amalfi.

FASHION

Naples is *the* fashion capital of southern Italy. The popular fashion shopping streets are the Via Toledo and the Chiaia quarter *(Via Chiaia, Via Calabritto, Via dei Mille)*. A classic is *Marinella (Riviera di Chiaia 287 | www.marinellanapoli.it)*, where they make the most elegant ties in the city. You can also find the perfect shirt to match.

HANDICRAFTS

Every city district, every place in Campania has over many generations specialised in a particular craft. For example in the *centro storico* of Naples along the Spaccanapoli there are streets full of jewellery stores, streets selling musical instruments, streets just with bookstores, streets with stationery stores, shops that only sell artificial flowers made from paper, wax, silk, or streets with only antique shops. There is even a whole street that is exclusively dedicated to nativity scenes, the Via San Gregorio Armeno, which transforms into a colourful bazaar during Christmas time. Positano on the Amalfi Coast creates its own summer fashion made from colourful, light fabrics, while the rather chaotic coastal town of Torre del Greco is the hub of the coral, cameo, shell and gemstone jewellery world. The oldest manufacture of coral (Ascione, founded in 1855) has opened an extensive INSIDER TIP *Museo del Corallo (Galleria Umberto I 19 | www.ascione.it)* in Naples.

Ceramics, corals, culinary delights: each place, each neighbourhood maintains their owns crafts and traditions

In Amalfi and Tramonti, the tradition of making fine paper has survived and the paper makes a wonderful souvenir, as it is easy to transport. And in Sorrento the art of wood inlays still thrives: there are boxes and chests, trays, frames and much more. Ceramic and majolica vases and crockery have been traditionally crafted on the coast (Vietri sul Mare) and on the region's islands (Ischia). The overwhelming scents of blossoms and herbs which fill the air on the island of Capri have inspired many of the aromatic perfumes manufactured in the Carthusia Laboratory on Capri using local essential oils extracted from petals.. San Leucio is a village in Caserta that developed around silk manufacturing; there are still eight factories here today where you can purchase the most beautiful silk fabrics.

MARKETS

Whether you want to shop or to people watch, the markets here are always a pleasure. You will find colourful daily street markets in Naples (www.napoli davivere.it) at the Porta Nolana and the Pignasecca that are full of vegetables, fruit, fish, clothes and household appliances. Then there are also the antique and flea markets held every third weekend of the month at the Villa Comunale city park and huge daily second-hand market on the Corsa Resina in Ercolano, a treasure trove for clothes from the 1970s.

NAPLES SOUVENIRS

In Napolimania at no. 312 Via Toledo you can find souvenirs which play off the clichés of Naples: graffiti slogans or a can of "Aria di Napoli" (air of Naples). This shop is the perfect place to find cheeky, offbeat pop culture items that are a world away from the flower fragrances of Capri. How about a little red horn, an amulet used for protection from the malocchio, the evil eye?

NAPLES

MAP INSIDE BACK COVER
(133 D 4–5) (*C–D4*) **You may be a little nervous before your visit to the city. Will you find your way around in the chaos? Will you still have your handbag and camera when you get home?**

Being cautious is always advisable, the police also know this and so they have regular patrols in the historic town centre of Naples and around the tourist attractions. Despite the gritty chaos and grime there is also the warm friendliness of the locals, hearty laughter, leafy squares, the radiant blue of sky and sea, the aroma of *caffè*, sweet pastries and pizza, sweeping grandeur and deeply rooted cultural awareness. Naples also has a very modern urban side with some glass and steel skyscrapers in the east of the city, and there is a penchant for contemporary art in squares, in the Metro stations, in new museums and trendy galleries.

Napoli, the Campania region's capital city, is Italy's third largest city. The population density is ten times greater than that of Florence, with 1 million inhabitants, but it swells to 3 million when the sprawling metropolitan area outside the city limit is included. There are some 300 churches, numerous palaces, castles and monasteries tucked away within the city. Each era, each regime, has left behind its insignia: medieval fortresses and Gothic churches, whom the splendour of the baroque of the Counter-Reformation gave a new facelift. In the 18th century, when Naples was one of Europe's most magnificent and important cities, the "good" Kin

Fortresses, catacombs and the sweet life:
Italy's third largest city is as fascinating above
ground as it is below its (shifting) ground

CITY WHERE TO START?

From the **Piazza Trieste e Trento (U D5)** (*f5*) it is easy to explore on foot in all directions: to the Piazza del Plebiscito next door, shopping in the Chiaia quarter or through the Via Toledo pedestrian zone via the Piazza Dante to the *centro storico* in 30 minutes. Get there by bus R 2 from the main station.

Charles commissioned the sumptuous San Carlo Theatre, the grand royal palaces of Capodimonte, Caserta and Portici and last but not least he also built the massive Albergo dei Poveri (hostel for the poor).

The best way to explore the quaint, historical city centre – with its sightseeing attractions tucked away in a maze of alleyways – is on foot. The transport links are not indicated due to the nature of the sightseeing attractions. Buses (C 57, R 2, R 4) travel along the arterial roads

Castel Nuovo, the "new" castle, is over 700 years old

that flank the old town. The cable railway connects the city's high-lying districts. The long, straight *Spaccanapoli* splits the *centro storico* in two parts (*spaccare* = split) called Via Benedetto Croce/Via San Biagio dei Librai on the map.

Another orientation guide is the *Via Toledo*, a grand boulevard during the time of the Spanish viceroys and today one of the city's main shopping streets: from the former Reggia Capodimonte it leads down towards the sea and flanks the chaotic district of Sanità to the left, Quartieri Spagnoli to the right. Then the Via Toledo touches the historic old town at the Piazza Dante and reaches the Palazzo Reale at the Piazza del Plebiscito at its end.

The Santa Lucia neighbourhood is at the seaside; from the coastal roads Via Nazario Sauro and Via Partenope the large, luxurious traditional hotels look out on to the rock fortification of the Castel dell'Ovo. In the north and west of the city, is the wide open area of "Napoli bene", the upper middle-class *Chiaia San Ferdinando* with stately homes and apartments and a few nice hotels, fine shops, the elegant Piazza dei Martiri and many trendy restaurants or the more anonymous district of *Vomero* which lies higher up, with its popular Piazza Vanvitelli and the wonderful ☆ *Posillipo* with its villas overlooking the sea. Old aristocratic buildings and villas often line the street, so look at their handsomely framed portals – you may catch a glimpse of the wonderful courtyards and stairways within.

SIGHTSEEING

CAPPELLA SANSEVERO (U E2) *(∅ g3)*
The Neapolitan cult of the dead finds its aesthetic high point in the marble-veiled Christ by Giuseppe Sammartino (1753) in the rococo chapel of the nobleman and alchemist Raimondo di Sangro. In the crypt you will find the remains of a macabre experiment: the petrified arterial network of two deceased people, presumably serv-

ants, whose veins were apparently injected by Raimondo with a hardening liquid while they were alive. *Mon and Wed–Sat 9.30am–5630pm, Sun 9.30am–2pm | Via F. De Sanctis 19 | www.museo sansevero.it*

CASTEL NUOVO (U D–E4) *(ⓂⓊ f–g5)*

Built at the end of the 13th century by Charles I of Anjou, therefore also called *Maschio Angioino*. The wonderful *Renaissance arch* is impressive. *Mon–Sat 9am–7pm | Piazza Municipio*

CASTEL DELL'OVO/BORGO MARINARI 🌿 (U D6) *(ⓂⓊ f7)*

A mythical place on the small island Megaride: Vergil is meant to have built an egg into the walls of the castle *(Mon–Sat 9am–7.30pm, Sun 9am–2pm)*, and according to legend Naples will stay standing as long as this egg remains intact. At the foot of the castle is the *Borgo Marinari*, once a fishing

village, today a lively meeting place with cafés and exclusive restaurants. *Buses R 3, 140*

CASTEL SANT'ELMO 🌿 (U C3) *(ⓂⓊ d–e4)*

You can enjoy the best view of the *centro storico* from the third castle, a star-shaped fortress from the Anjou era at the eastern edge of the Vomero plateau. Today unusual art exhibitions take place here in some of the rooms. In front of the castle is the Carthusian monastery *Certosa di San Martino* (today a museum, see p. 38). *Wed–Mon 9am–7pm | Via Tito Angelini | www.polomusealenapoli.beniculturali.it | Funicolare Montesanto*

DUOMO SAN GENNARO (U E–F2) *(ⓂⓊ g–h2)*

The interior of the cathedral which has been richly decorated over the centuries has a splendid baroque chapel that houses the blood reliquary (in an am-

---

⭐ **Museo e Gallerie Nazionali di Capodimonte**
The rich art collection is considered to be the "Louvre at Vesuvius" → p. 37

⭐ **Napoli Sotterranea**
Naples' underworld: Roman quarries, Greek cisterns, baroque wells, war bunkers and Camorra hideouts → p. 38

⭐ **Galleria Borbonica**
Once an escape route for the Neapolitan king, now an adventure playground for adults → p. 36

⭐ **Kayak tours in Posillipo**
Explore the city on water to gain a whole new perspective → p. 43

⭐ **Museo Nazionale di San Martino**
The monastery's collection of nativity scenes and the stunning views from the belvedere → p. 38

⭐ **Museo Archeologico Nazionale**
Magnificent mosaics and paintings from Pompeii, masterpieces of ancient sculpture → p. 37

⭐ **Metro stations**
Do not miss out on taking the underground line 1, the *Metrò dell'Arte* → p. 37

⭐ **Cuma**
Home of the famous Greek oracle Sibyl. A beautiful *passeggiata* leads to the acropolis hill → p. 47

MARCO POLO HIGHLIGHTS

poule) of the city's patron saint San Gennaro, which miraculously liquefies ● thrice a year, on 19 September, 12 December and on the Saturday before the first Sunday in May. The *excavations (Mon–Sat 8.30am–1.30pm and 2.30pm–8pm, Sun 8.30am–1.30pm and 4.30pm–7.30pm, shorter times in August)* below the cathedral show the remnants of Greek, Roman and medieval Naples. In the *cathedral museum (daily 9am–*

Óscar Tusquets Blanca's mosaic "Crater de Luz" in the Toledo metro station

5.30pm | www.museosangennaro.it) the cathedral's treasures are displayed. *Via Duomo*

GALLERIA BORBONICA ★
(U C5–6) (*𝄞 e6*)
This series of tunnels once used by the Neapolitan king to escape the city now exhibits relicts dumped underground over the centuries including old cars and motorbikes from 1930 to 1960. Those with a head for adventure should take the *percorso avventura* tour where you will be equipped with a helmet and climbing gear. *Fri–Sun 10am, noon, 3.30pm, 5.30pm | Via Domenico Morelli 40 | www.galleriaborbonica.com*

GALLERIA UMBERTO I (U D4) (*𝄞 f5*)
The elegant shopping arcade with its big glass dome is typical of the late 19th century. *Via Toledo/Via San Carlo*

GESÙ NUOVO (U D3) (*𝄞 f3*)
Gesù Nuovo was the church of the Jesuits in Naples. Built in 1584, it is a powerful example of Neapolitan baroque style. The diamond shapes on its façade are unusual; the façade is a remnant of the original palace. *Piazza del Gesù Nuovo*

CATACOMBS ●
Behind the Basilica della Madre del Buon Consiglio, frescos lead down to the entrance of the underground cemetery of the early Christians, the *Catacombe di San Gennaro (Tue–Sun 10am–5pm, Sun 10am–1pm every hour on the hour | Via Capodimonte 13 (0) (𝄞 0) | www.catacombedinapoli.it | bus M 5 from Metro Museo, R 4 from Piazza Dante)*. Not far away are some more catacombs, under the Santa Maria della Sanità church: *Catacombe di San Gaudosio (daily every hour on the hour 10am–1pm | (0) (𝄞 f1))*. They date to the 5th century BC. A **INSIDER TIP** small bone vault *(Mon–Sat 10am–2pm | Via dei Tribunali 39 (U E2) (𝄞 g2))* can be found below the *Santa Maria delle Anime del Purgatorio ad Arco Church* in the old town.
The ⊙ **INSIDER TIP** *La Paranza* cultural cooperative *(www.catacombedinapoli.it/it/about)* not only accompanies visitors to the catacombs, but also offers

city tours *(bookable in Italian/English via prenotazioi@catacombedinapoli.it)* and educates visitors about the social conditions in the troubled Sanità district and suggests intelligent solutions, offering the youth career prospects and alternatives to the Camorra and a life of crime.

MADRE AND PAN

These abbreviations represent the two exciting collections of contemporary art in the stylishly restored *palazzi* in the heart of the old town. In the *Museo d'Arte Contemporanea Donna Regina (Mon and Wed–Sat 10am–7.30pm, Sun 10am–8pm | Via Settembrini 79* (U E1) *(𝄞 g1)* | *www.madrenapoli.it*) some of the works from the international art elite of the past 50 years are on show – including Joseph Beuys, Andy Warhol, Richard Serra, Jeff Koons and Mimmo Paladino. And with the *Palazzo delle Arti di Napoli (Mon and Wed–Sat 9.30am–7.30pm, Sun 9.30am–2.30pm | Via dei Mille 60* (U B5) *(𝄞 d5)* | *www.palazzoartinapoli. net* | *buses C 22, C 24, C 25, C 28)*, the forum for new, vibrant art from Naples, the city has connected to the cultural present.

METRO STATIONS ⭐ ●

The new underground line 1 connects eleven stations exhibiting impressive works of art. The award-winning stations Toledo, Dante and Museo have been designed by artists including William Kentridge, Jannis Kounellis, Robert Wilson, Oliviero Toscani and Joseph Kosuth and are the most attractive. Visitors can enjoy some of the finest works of contemporary art for the price of a metro ticket and there is a free guided tour every Wednesday at 10.30am (only in Italian at the time of going to print) through the art stations.

MUSEO ARCHEOLOGICO NAZIONALE ⭐ (U D1) *(𝄞 f2)*

The museum has an unparalleled collection of ancient Mediterranean art and artefacts from the 8th century BC to the 5th century AD. The collection was assembled in the second half of the 18th century, a time when interest in ancient archaeology and art was at its peak in Europe. Naples was the centre of this interest with its excavations at Herculaneum and Pompeii. Some of the highlights from Pompeii, Herculaneum and Stabiae include the sculptures, the elaborate mosaics and frescos and the wonderfully delicate landscape and portrait paintings from Pompeian villas. Visitors over 12 years are allowed into the *Gabinetto Segreto*, a collection of erotic illustrations from Pompeii's pleasure houses which were kept under lock and key for many years – well-executed and quite unambiguous! After visiting the museum the Art nouveau *Galleria Principe di Napoli* is the ideal place for a stroll or a bite to eat. *Wed–Mon 9am–7.30pm | Piazza Museo | cir.campania.beniculturali.it/museoar cheologiconazionale*

MUSEO DELLE ARTI SANITARIE (U E2) *(𝄞 g2)*

An originally preserved pharmacy dating back to the 18th century with majolica vessels and a museum tracing the medical history of the Ospedale degli Incurabili hospital which is still open today. *Mon–Fri 9.30am–1.30pm, pharmacy only Sat with pre-booking | Via Maria Longo 50 | tel. 0 81 44 06 47 | www.museoartisanitarie.it*

MUSEO E GALLERIE NAZIONALI DI CAPODIMONTE ⭐ ⚘ (0) *(𝄞 0)*

Situated high above the city, the chaste red-grey palace houses the high calibre collection of paintings of the Bourbon kings by Italian masters such as Titian,

Mantegna, Caravaggio and many others, by Dutch masters such as Pieter Brueghel, in short: one of the richest galleries in Italy. The highlight is a salon made entirely from porcelain, a work of the legendary porcelain manufacturer Capodimonte. In the well-maintained 🔆 park full of palm trees families go for walks on Sundays. Behind the park is an expansive forest, the city's green lung and a jogger's paradise. *Thu–Tue 8.30am–7.30pm | Via Miano 2 | cir.campaniabeni culturali.it/museodicapodimonte | bus R 4 from Piazza Dante, bus M 5 from Metro Museo*

MUSEO NAZIONALE DELLA CERAMICA DUCA DI MARTINA (U A4) *(𝄞 c5)*
In the middle of this wonderful Villa Floridiana park on the Vomero lies this classical villa full of precious treasures made from porcelain, glass, ivory and corals. There is also a wonderful view of the Gulf and islands from the park's 🔆 belvedere. *Wed–Mon 8am–2pm, park daily 9am–1 hour before sunset | Via Cimarosa 77 | cir.campaniabeniculturali. it /floridiana | Funicolare Chiaia*

MUSEO NAZIONALE DI SAN MARTINO ★ 🔆 (U C3) *(𝄞 e4)*
The views, the garden, the fantastic Neapolitan nativity scenes as well as the historical views of Naples and the Gulf: all excellent reasons to visit the impressive San Martino Carthusian monastery, easily accessible with the cable car. *Thu–Tue 8.30am–7.30pm | Largo San Martino | cir. campania.beniculturali.it/museosanmar tino | Funicolare Montesanto*

NAPOLI SOTTERRANEA (NAPLES UNDERGROUND) ★ ● (U E3) *(𝄞 e3)*
Here you descend into the city's underworld: a labyrinth of tunnels, cisterns, storage cellars, sewerage systems and caves, which were cut into the soft volcanic lava by the Greeks and Romans. The quarries later served as landfills and as air raid shelters during the war. A little oddity: descending into remnants of a Roman theatre. *Daily 10am–6pm every hour on the hour, guided tours in English 10am, noon, 2pm, 4pm, 6pm | Piazza San Gaetano 68 | www.napolisotterranea.org*

PALAZZO DELLO SPAGNOLO (U E1) *(𝄞 g1)*
In Rione Sanità, one of the more chaotic districts in the historic centre, there are some very interesting examples of the bold, late baroque architecture of the great architect Ferdinando Sanfelice (1675–1748). His signature was the *scale aperte*, sweeping open double ramp staircases, especially the one at this Palazzo. *Largo dei Vergini 19*

PIAZZA DANTE (U D2) *(𝄞 f3)*
The fresh winds of urban renewal have been blowing over this semi-circular piazza. Signs of change include the new art Metro station and the INSIDER TIP renowned avant-garde gallery *Fondazione Morra (Mon–Fri 10am–5pm, Sat 10am–1.30pm | www.fondazionemorra.org)* in the Palazzo Ruffo di Bagnara. Behind the Dante statue the Via Port'Alba leads you past bookstores to the Piazza Bellini into the *centro storico*. In the narrow streets above the Piazza Dante is the 🔆 *Museo Hermann Nitsch (Sept–July Mon–Fri 10am–7pm, Sat 10am–2pm | Vico Lungo Pontecorvo 29 d | www.museonitsch.org)* in an old power station, the ideal exhibition space for the Austrian performance artist.

PIAZZA DEL PLEBISCITO/PALAZZO REALE (U D5) *(𝄞 f5)*
The impressive royal palace, the *Palazzo Reale (Thu–Tue 9am–8pm | www.palaz zorealenapoli.it)* is on the neoclassical

Piazza del Plebiscito, a parade and fairground in the 19th century. It was built at the beginning of the 17th century by Domenico Fontana at the time of the Spanish viceroys. In 1727 the magnificent staircase was constructed. In the palace complex are chambers, a court theatre and a collection of paintings and

vehicle-free area is now a popular meeting place for the locals as well as visitors. Every year at Christmas the square becomes a massive outdoor gallery, where internationally renowned artists such as Mimmo Paladino, Anish Kapoor, Rebecca Horn, Richard Serra or Carsten Nicolai have created impressive instal-

The neoclassical Piazza del Plebiscito with the San Francesco di Paola Church

gardens to view. Opposite is *San Francesco di Paola*, a 19th century domed church based on the design of the Pantheon. During the Bourbon reign the Piazza was the stage for a Neapolitan variant of the Roman "bread and circus" games where the hungry crowds were allowed to grab from a mountain of groceries on certain days. Such an occasion could be a royal wedding, an important religious ceremony or a threatened revolt. The piazza was a litter strewn *parcheggio* (car park) until the 1990s; today the square is a symbol of the city's cultural rebirth. The

lations. And the New Year's Eve rave on the Piazza Plebiscito is a mega event that one simply has to experience!

PIO MONTE DELLA MISERICORDIA
(U F2) (*m h2*)

The welfare organisation, which is still active today, was founded by seven Neapolitan nobles in 1601 and it is the home of the altarpiece "The Seven Works of Mercy" created in 1607 by the Baroque genius Caravaggio. *Daily 9am–2pm | Via Tribunali 253 | www.piomontedellami sericordia.it*

POSILLIPO AND MARECHIARO
(O) (*₪ a7*)

Along the Gulf of Naples towards the south-west is the exclusive ﹏ *Posillipo* residential district: refuge of the city's wealthy residents, the nouveau rich and the old aristocratic families, who left their volcanic rock to the sea. The *Parco Sommerso di Gaiola (Tue–Sun 10am–2pm, summer until 4pm | www.areamarinapro tettagaiola.it)* protects the area's archaeological and environmental heritage. The ﹏ bus route 140 runs along the Posillipo coast.

Majolica splendour among citrus trees: cloister at the Santa Chiara monastery

palaces behind in the chaotic city a long time ago. The villas are set in enchanted gardens sloping down to the sea on the foothills of Monte Posillipo and the semi derelict, romantic ruin ﹏ *Palazzo Donn' Anna* is right on the seaside. Everything is very private, even access to the sea. There are a few public, exclusive bathing beaches. The former fishing village of Marechiaro ajoins Posillipo and offers some romantic ﹏ seafood restaurants with superb views over the Gulf, e.g. *Da Cicciotto (daily | Calata Ponticello a Marechiaro 32 | tel.08 15 75 11 65 | www. trattoriadacicciotto.it | Expensive)*. Also impressive is the 700m long tunnel, *Grotta di Seiano* that runs through the

SAN LORENZO MAGGIORE
(U E2) (*₪ g2*)

A stately church in the French Gothic style. The *excavations (Mon–Sat 9.30am– 5.30pm, Sun 9.30am–1.30pm | www. sanlorenzomaggiore.na.it)* under the church, discovered in the second half of the 20th century, are especially worth seeing. They reveal parts of the Roman city, built on Greek wall ruins, that include a well-preserved Roman market street with bakery, wine pub and the remnants of a market square. *Piazza San Gaetano*

SANTA CHIARA (U D–E3) (*₪ f–g3*)
Badly damaged in the 1943 bomb raids, the impressive monastery church was re-

built in its original French Gothic style. The interior is the burial place for numerous kings and aristocrats and includes Robert of Anjou's grave which has the largest tombstone from the Middle Ages. In the courtyard of the cloister is the magical *Chiostro delle Clarisse,* a monastery garden with majolica tiled benches, fragrant lemon and orange trees and beautiful porticos. In the anteroom to the garden you can admire a massive nativity scene from the 18th/19th century. *Mon–Sat 9.30am–5.30pm, Sun 10am–2.30pm | Via Benedetto Croce/Via Santa Chiara 49c | www.monasterodisantachiara.com*

TEATRO SAN CARLO (U D5) *(ψ f5)*
Europe's oldest opera house, built in 1737 as a court theatre for the Neapolitan king Charles and still offering an international, prestigious programme. *Guided tours daily 10.30am, 11.30am, 12.30pm and Mon–Sat 2.30pm, 3.30pm, 4.30pm | Via San Carlo 98f | www.teatrosancarlo.it*

FOOD & DRINK

CAFÉS, PASTICCERIE, GELATERIE
The most traditional café is without a doubt ● *Gran Caffè Gambrinus (Piazza Trieste e Trento* (U D5) *(ψ f5)); here you can also get the best puff pastry sfogliatelle.* Important examples of Neapolitan 19th century art adorn the walls of the big hall. During the summer time you sit at the cafés in the *Borgo Marinari* (U D6) *(ψ f6)*, very chic is the *Gran Caffè La Caffettiera* at the pretty *Piazza dei Martiri* (U C5) *(ψ e6)* in Chiaia, very trendy is the *S'Move-Lab (Vico dei Sospiri 10a* (U C5) *(ψ e6)):* Thu–Sun DJs play house, funk and acid jazz while guests enjoy their aperitifs.
Naples' most famous *pasticcerie* or pastry shops are *Scaturchio (Piazza San Domenico Maggiore* (U E2) *(ψ g3))* and *Leopoldo (Via Chiaia 258* (U D5) *(ψ f5)).*

This shop also sells spicy *taralli,* a peppery snack with almonds.
Donalfredon 1946 (U D2) *(ψ f3)* is a traditional juice bar on the Piazza Dante serving freshly squeezed orange juice and lemonade as well as a INSIDER TIP delicious apple juice made from the Neapolitan cultivar of apple, *mela annurca.* The Neapolitans meet up late into the night at the ice cream parlours on the shores of Mergellina (0) *(ψ 0)*, especially at the ● *Chalet Ciro (Via Caracciolo).*

DA GINO SORBILLO ● (U E2) *(ψ g2)*
Legendary pizzeria from the 1950s which has launched the success of a new star pizza baker, grandson Gino. *Closed Sun | Via dei Tribunali 32 | tel. 0 81 44 66 43 | www. sorbillo.it | Budget*

DA GIOVANNI (0) *(ψ 0)*
Trattoria in the third generation near the old fish market. Serves fresh fish in a warm atmosphere. *Closed Sun | Via Soprammuro a Nolana 9 | tel. 0 81 26 83 20 | Budget*

MANGIAFOGLIA (U B5) *(ψ d5)*
Stylish and creative dishes for vegetable lovers – the Neapolitans were given the nickname "leaf eaters" *(mangiafoglia)* in the 18th century due to their affinity for vegetables. *Closed Sun | Via Giosuè Carducci 32 | tel. 0 81 41 46 31 | Moderate–Expensive*

LA MATTONELLA (U C5) *(ψ e5)*
The epitome of a family-run trattoria: red and white chequered tablecloths and traditional homemade dishes such as *pasta alla genovese. Closed Sun | Via Giovanni Nicotera 13 | tel. 0 81 41 65 41 | Budget–Moderate*

NENNELLA (U D3) *(ψ f4)*
A lively, noisy and simple trattoria with a cult following. *Closed Sun | Vico Lungo*

LE SORELLE BANDIERA (U E2) (*ω g2*)
This pizzeria serves "geothermal pizza" as known by the ancient Romans where the dough is left to rise slowly in tuff stone caves and then baked in a tuff stone oven. *Closed Mon evening | Vico Cinquesanti 33 | tel. 0 81 19 50 35 35 | www.lesorellebandiera.com | Budget*

INSIDER TIP ▶ SORRISO INTEGRALE ⊕ (U D2) (*ω f2–3*)
Located in a courtyard behind the Piazza Bellini, this landmark organic restaurant (many organic home-grown Demeter ingredients) also has a vegetarian menu. *Daily | Vico San Pietro a Maiella 6 | tel. 0 81 45 50 26 | www.sorriointegrale.com | Budget*

INSIDER TIP ▶ TANDEM (U E2) (*ω g3*)
Young, cult restaurant specialising in the Neapolitan Sunday lunch classic, ragù where meat is braised in tomato sauce and served with bread or pasta. Vegetarian option is also available. *Closed Wed | Via Giovanni Paladino 51 | tel. 0 81 19 00 24 68 | www.tandem.napoli.it | Budget*

Stylish shopping in the elegant Galleria Umberto I

Teatro Nuovo 105 | tel. 0 81 41 43 38 | Budget

PALAZZO PETRUCCI (U E2) (*ω g3*)
Contemporary fine-dining restaurant with new interpretations of Neapolitan cuisine. Excellent selection of wines. *Closed Sun evening and Mon lunchtime. | Piazza San Domenico Maggiore 4 | tel. 08 15 52 40 68 | www.palazzopetrucci.it | Expensive*

SHOPPING

A tourist highlight (and not only during Christmas) are the shops and workshops selling nativity scenes along the *Via San Gregorio Armeno* (U E2) (*ω g2–3*). The exclusive fashion boutiques (all (U C5) (*ω e5–6*)) are found along the *Via Chiaia, Via dei Mille, Via Calabritto* and *Piazza dei Martiri* in Chiaia San Ferdinando as well as the *Galleria Umberto I (Via Toledo/Via San Carlo* (U D4) (*ω f5*)). In addition to boutiques there are plenty of neighbourhood markets. The *food market* at the *Piazza Pignasecca* (U D3) (*ω f3*) is very traditional, while the epitome of an Neapolitan *mercato popolare* is the *fish market* at the

Porta Nolana (0) (*µ 0*). Very traditional: the handmade umbrellas sold at ● *Talarico (Vico Due Porte a Toledo 4b* (U D3) (*µ f4*) | *www.mariotalarico.it)* in the Quartieri Spagnoli. Traditional and contemporary Napoli sounds – at the trendy *lounge bar Fonoteca (closed Mon | Via Raffaele Morghen 31c/f* (U B3) (*µ d4*) | *tel. 08 15 56 03 38* | *www.fonoteca.net)* in the Vomero district, the upmarket area on a hill in Naples. Trendy locals, hip cocktails and plenty of nightlife tips. There are also lots of well-stocked CD stores in the *centro storico*.

LEISURE & SPORTS

BICYCLES

With a modest pool of 100 bikes, the bike-sharing concept is emerging as a popular transport option even in Naples. *www.bikesharingnapoli.it*

KAYAK TOURS IN POSILLIPO ★ ⬐ (0) (*µ 0*)

This is a unique way of discovering this spectacular section of coastline with its Roman remains. Sail past the haunted (according to the legend) antique palace, Palazzo degli Spiriti, to the old fishing bay of Borgo Marechiaro. The tour lasts 2 to 3 hours and a visit to the private beach nearby is also included in the price of *30 euros. Via Posillipo 68 (entrance to the Lido Le Rocce Verdi beach)* | *tel. 33 88 76 11 57* | *www.kayaknapoli.com* | *bus 140 from Metro Mergellina*

TERME DI AGNANO ● (0) (*µ 0*)

Historical thermal baths with natural steam grottos. *Mon–Sat 7.30am–1pm and 2.30pm–5.30pm | Via Agnano Astroni 24 | www.termediagnano.it | buses C 2 and C 6 from Campi Flegrei station on the Ferrovia Cumana*

ENTERTAINMENT

The warm evenings are ideal for strolling and eating ice cream at the seafront promenade, the *lungomare*. The freaks sit on the *Piazza San Domenico Maggiore* (U E2) (*µ f2–3*) in the old town while the tourists, students and intellectuals gather around the INSIDERTIP ▶ *Piazza Bellini* (U D2) (*µ f2–3*). A nightlife scene has developed in the Chiaia district around the *Piazza dei Martiri* (U C5) (*µ e6*), in the Vomero people meet up at the *Vintage Wine Bar (Via Gian Lorenzo Bernini 37a* (U A3) (*µ c4*)) near the Piazza Vanvitelli. An excellent classic among the music clubs with live music is *Up Stroke (Via Coroglio 128* (0) (*µ 0*)) in Bagnoli. Summer discos can be found on the beaches of Bacoli, Pozzuoli and Baia. Some restaurants offer Neapolitan live music on weekends, such as the pleasant *Salone Margherita (Via Santa Brigida 65/66* (U D4) (*µ f5*) | *www.salonemargherita.net)*.
An uplifting experience is an opera, a concert or a ballet in the magnificent *Teatro San Carlo (tickets Mon–Sat 10am–5.30pm | Via San Carlo 98 f* (U D5) (*µ f5*) | *tel. 08 17 97 24 68* | *www.teatrosancarlo.it)*. Some churches and *palazzi* are also the venues for classical concerts such as the INSIDERTIP ▶ excellent concerts of ancient Neapolitan music by *Centro Musica Antica Pietà de' Turchini* in the *Santa Caterina da Siena* church *(Via Santa Caterina da Siena 38* (U C4) (*µ e5*) | *tel. 0 81 40 23 95* | *www.turchini.it)*. Programme information in the daily press, e.g. in "Il Mattino".

WHERE TO STAY

More and more owners of large old town apartments now offer stylish bed & breakfast accommodation *(Budget–Moderate)*, a great way to get to know the city in a more personal way. *www.bb-napoli.com, www.*

bed-breakfast.napoli.it, www.rentabed.it, www.bed-and-breakfast.it/it/napoli

B&B CAPPELLA VECCHIA
(U C5) (*M e6*)
In Chiaia near the Piazza dei Martiri, six comfortable, modern rooms, freshly baked *sfogliatelle* for breakfast. *Vico Santa Maria a Cappella Vecchia 11 | tel. 08 12 40 51 17 | www.cappellavecchia11.it | Budget–Moderate*

INSIDER TIP ▶ B&B CASA DEL MONACONE ⦿ (0) (*M f1*)
A B&B run by the cultural initiative La Paranza in a restored former monastery next to Chiesa Santa Maria della Sanità, a contribution to the social uplifting of the problem Sanità district. Meet interesting people from all over the world. *7 rooms | Via Sanità 124 |tel. 08 17 44 37 14 | www.casadelmonacone.it | bus R 4, Ascensore della Sanità | Budget*

CHIAJA HOTEL DE CHARME
(U D5) (*M f5*)
On the first floor of an inner city *palazzo* near the Piazza del Plebiscito with the atmosphere and the charming grandeur of an exclusive home. *27 rooms | Via Chiaia 216 | tel. 0 81 41 55 55 | www.chiaiahotel.com | Moderate*

COSTANTINOPOLI 104 (U D2) (*M f2*)
An oasis in the midst of the city chaos: charming hotel in a villa with lovely garden and swimming pool near Piazza Bellini. *19 rooms | Via Santa Maria di Costantinopoli 104 | tel. 08 15 57 10 35 | www.costantinopoli104.com | Moderate–Expensive*

CULTURE HOTEL CENTRO STORICO
(U D3) (*M f4*)
Functional, modern hotel in the middle of the old part of the city. *24 rooms | Via Monteoliveto 15 | tel. 08 15 52 94 35 | centrostorico.culturehotel.it | Moderate*

HOSTEL OF THE SUN (U E4) (*M g4*)
Friendly and clean, with self-catering kitchen. Five 3, 4 and 6 bed dorms, one double room. *Via Melisurgo 15 | tel. 08 14 20 63 93 | www.hostelnapoli.com | Budget*

NAPOLIT'AMO PRINCIPE AND MEDINA
Two hostels under the same management: the *Principe* on the first floor of an old city *palazzo (13 rooms | Via Toledo 148 | bus R 2 | tel. 08 15 52 36 26 | www.napolitamo.it | Budget)*, the *Napolit'amo* near the town hall *(17 rooms | Via San Tommaso d'Aquino 15 | tel. 08 14 97 71 10 | www.napolitamo.it | bus R 2 | Budget–Moderate)*.

PALAZZO ALABARDIERI (U C5) (*M e6*)
Fine hotel housed in a restored *palazzo* in the elegant Chiaia district. *35 rooms | Via Alabardieri 38 | tel. 0 81 41 52 78 | www.palazzoalabardieri.it | Expensive*

ROMEO (U E4) (*M g4*)
Innovative, luxury hotel designed by the Japanese architect Kenzo Tange on the harbour with sushi bar, 1000m^2 spa and a ✦ starred restaurant with views of Mount Vesuvius. *83 rooms | Via Cristoforo Colombo 45 | tel. 08 10 17 50 01 | www.romeohotel.it | Expensive*

FERRIES

Boats to Capri, Ischia and Procida as well as to Sorrento depart from *Calata Porta di Massa* ((U F3–4) (*M h4*), car ferries), from the *Molo Beverello* ((U E5) (*M g5*), hydrofoils), the *Porto Turistico Mergellina* ((0) (*M b7*, only Ischia and Procida) and from *Pozzuoli* ((132 C5) (*M C4*), car ferries and hydrofoils). In the summer additional hydrofoils *(www.metrodelmare.net)* service Naples and the towns on the coasts of Amalfi and Cilento. Information and schedules are listed in the free brochure "Qui Napoli" and in the "Il Mattino" or "La Repubblica" daily newspapers.

INFORMATION

CITY OF NAPLES
Piazza del Gesù 7 | (U D3) *(↳ f3), tel. 08 15 51 27 01 | www.inaples.it; Via San Carlo 9* (U D4–5) *(↳ f5) | tel. 0 81 40 23 94).* You can get the free information brochure "Qui Napoli" everywhere in Italian/

(↳ e6) | *tel. 0 81 410 72 11* | *www.eptnapoli.info*

WHERE TO GO

CAMPI FLEGREI (PHLEGRAEAN FIELDS)
(132 B–C 4–5) *(↳ B–C4)*
Even if the "burning fields" about 15 km/9 miles west of Naples no longer steam and hiss everywhere, the Solfatara of Pozzuoli, hydrothermal lakes, ruins and damaged buildings all clearly illustrate the seismic activity in the area. The Campi Flegrei are easily accessible by public transport, you can either take the Metro or the Ferrovia Cumana e Circumflegrea train from Naples.

Japan at the foot of Mount Vesuvius: spend the night in Feng-Shui rooms at the Romeo Hotel

English which lists the current opening times of the sightseeing attractions, exhibition times, schedules of the ferries and commuter trains.

PROVINCE OF NAPLES AND ISLANDS
At the main train station (0) *(↳ 0)* | *tel. 0 81 26 87 79; Piazza dei Martiri 58* (U C5)

The gritty housing developments around *Pozzuoli* (pop. 82,000) have some impressive ruins from the time when the city served as a Roman port: the ruins of the massive Roman market *Macellum,* where the pillars show the effects of the seismic phenomenon called bradyseism, the slow lifting and lowering of the earth's surface.

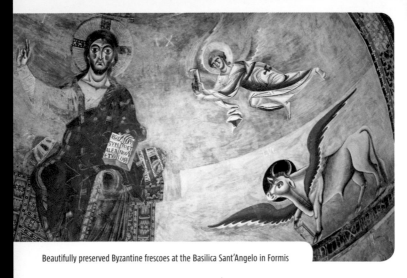
Beautifully preserved Byzantine frescoes at the Basilica Sant'Angelo in Formis

Also the massive *Anfiteatro Flavio (Wed–Mon 9am–2pm)* that dates back to AD 79. The seismic activity in the area meant that the picturesque and historic old town of Pozzuoli, which was located on a rocky hill, had to be vacated in 1970. Since then archaeological excavations at Rione Terra have uncovered a virtually intact Roman town *(Sat/Sun 9am–5pm | Via San Filippo 1f | www.campiflegreipark.it)*. At the eastern edge of the city is the *Solfatara (daily 8.30am–1 hr before sunset | Via Solfatara 161 | www.solfatara.it | bus 152 from Naples)*, a shallow 770 m/842 yds wide still active crater, with hot, bubbling mud puddles and steam vents *(fumarole)* which spew sulphurous gases. At the *Fumarola Bocca Grande* are the remains of a Roman thermal bath complex. In some places the ground is very hot and it is best to stay on the designated path.

The coastal road to the west leads along the 133 m/436 ft high *Monte Nuovo*, and the rather eerie *Lago d'Averno* crater lake. The mountain and lake form part of a nature reserve, making it ideal for hikes and picnics. In the south the Capo Miseno headland starts with the fishing village of *Baia*, in ancient times a fashionable resort, as evidenced by the Roman *spas (Parco Archeologico di Baia | Tue–Sun 9am–1 hr before sunset | Via Sella di Baia 22)*. There were once the luxurious bathing villas of the Roman elite all along the beach but they have since been swallowed by the sea. You can marvel at the ruins of the ancient walls and mosaic floors that litter the seabed from the glass-bottomed excursion boat, *Cymba (departures Sat noon, 3pm, Sun 10am, noon, 3pm | 10 euros | registration at info point at Baia harbour | tel. 34 94 97 41 83 | www.baiasommersa.it)*. From theory to practice: in the thermal bath ● *Stufe di Nerone (June–Aug daily 8am–8pm, Sept–May Tue, Thu and Fri 8am–11pm, Mon, Wed and Sat 8am–8pm, Sun 8am–6pm | Via Terme Stufe di Nerone 37 | www.terme stufedinerone.it)* you can relax in ancient steam grottos, or with freshly squeezed citrus juice in the quiet lemon tree garden. In the 16th century *castle (Tue–Sun 9am–2.20pm | museoarcheologicocampiflegrei.*

campaniabeniculturali.it), built on a Roman imperial villa, items from the villas and spas and statues that were found on the seabed are on show.

Behind Baia the freshwater *Lago del Fusaro* – which is separated from the sea by a narrow strip of land – spreads out. This is where the famous architect, Luigi Vanvitelli, built the hunting lodge *Casina del Fusaro* on the shores of the lake *(park daily 8am–8pm, Casina Sun 11am–1.30pm)*. In *Bacoli* further south the massive Roman *Piscina Mirabilis* is worth a visit *(daily 9am–1 hr before sunset | ask warden for entrance | tip)*, the largest preserved cistern from antiquity, which held about 12,000 cubic metres/445,000 cubic feet of water. Back towards the north, facing away from the *Capo Miseno* peninsula (beaches), you reach ★ ☞ *Cuma (daily 9am–2 hrs before sunset)*, the Greek Cumae (8th century BC), the first Greek colony on the mainland. Today it is a landscape of romantic ruins, perfectly located above the sea and shrouded in legend with the grotto of the Sibyl oracle (6th century BC). There are also the remains of an amphitheatre, an impressive defensive tunnel and an acropolis.

CAPUA/SANTA MARIA CAPUA VETERE
(133 D2) (*ω C–D2*)

In the little town of Capua (pop. 18,000, 33 km/20.5 miles north of Naples), a visit to the *Museo Campano (Tue–Sat 9am–1.30pm, Tue and Thu also 3pm–6pm, Sun 9am–1pm | Via Roma 68 | www.provincia.caserta.it/museocampano)* in the beautiful Palazzo Antignano is a must! It is has a rich collection of artefacts and works of art from antiquity and a very unique INSIDERTIP collection of votive statues in volcanic stone: mothers with babies in their arms (7th–1st century BC) from a nearby Italian *Mater Matuta* fertility shrine, which were excavated in 1870.

You can also see the impressive statues of the city gates of Capua, built by the Hohenstaufen emperor Frederick II.

6 km/3.7 miles to the north-east is the ☞ *Basilica Sant'Angelo in Formis (daily 9.30am–12.30pm and 3.30pm–7pm | www.diocesidicapua.it/basilicainformis)*, built in 1073. The interior is beautifully painted with INSIDERTIP medieval, well-preserved frescos. The tour continues to the enormous Roman *amphitheatre* of *Santa Maria Capua Vetere (Tue–Sun 9am–1 hr before sunset)* with its *Museo dei Gladiatori*. The most famous gladiator school, where Spartacus also learnt his craft, was here in Capua.

LOW BUDGET

☞ *Funicolari* offer an excellent overview: For only 1 euro, the rail cable car *(Montesanto* **(U C3)** *(ω e3)*, *Centrale* **(U D4)** *(ω f5)*, *Chiaia* **((U B4)** *(ω d5))* takes you to Vomero and a great view.

● The *monastery garden of San Gregorio Armeno* **((U E2)** *(ω g3)* | *Mon–Sat 9am–noon)* offers an oasis of calm in the midst of the city chaos. You need to ring the bell in order to be admitted, but there is no entrance fee (donations are welcome though).

Tasty, cheap and filling: *fritto misto* are the hot fried rice balls *(arancini)*, pastries filled with mozzarella *(panzarotti or rustici)* or fried zucchini that are available to take away for 2–5 euros, e.g. in the old town in *Da Matteo (Via dei Tribunali 94* **(U E2)** *(ω g2))* or at *Timpani e Tempura (Vico della Quercia 17* **U D3)** *(ω f3))*.

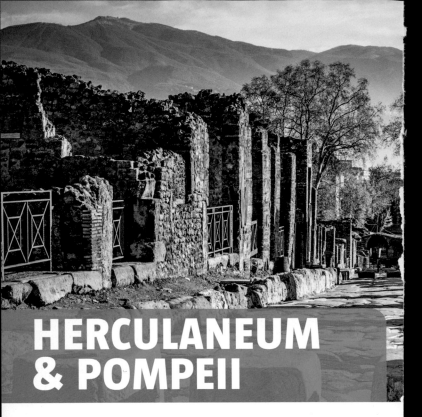

HERCULANEUM & POMPEII

More than 2 million people visit Pompeii every year, and every year the number increases – the same applies to Herculaneum. An onslaught that both these fragile ruined cities can hardly withstand, and they can barely keep abreast of the restoration work.

The entire attraction of Pompeii and Herculaneum lies in their fantastic condition, which illustrates in amazing detail the everyday life of the ancient Romans like no other site. The compelling sites bring to life a world that is 2000 years old and which, at other ruins, would only be experienced through tombs and their precious grave items or the remains of showpiece buildings. Here, however, you stroll through intact streets and alleys, lined with shops, workshops, bakeries and homes. The streets are paved with lava stone slabs, worn with deep grooves from the wagons of the ancients Romans and here and there you can still see the lead piping from the town's ancient aqueduct system, breaking through the pavements. Stucco decorations, frescos and remnants of mosaic floors all bear witness to a strong sense of beauty and aestheticism. The luminosity of the famous deep red of the Pompeii frescos is attributed to the fact that they added wax pigment with the limestone and soap solution and that the wall surface was smoothed with polished stones.

Leisure time was also an important aspect of everyday life: in addition to a few thea-

In the shadow of Mount Vesuvius: tangible evidence of everyday Roman life and two thousand year old villas

tres and the massive amphitheatre it is really the *palaestra* sport fields – where the young men played their sports – that attest to this. But there are also the public baths, the thermal spas and of course the *lupanare*, the brothels.

The eruption of Vesuvius began – after centuries of being dormant – on 24 August AD 79 with violent quakes. The summit of the mountain began to violently spew volcanic ash, massive dark clouds hung low, and in quick successive eruptions, glowing hot ash, boulders and *lapilli* (molten lava

hardened to pumice), all rained down on the cities that lay over 10 km/6 miles away. This was followed by two days of total darkness, until a pale light fought its way through the ash cloud and by the third day the sky cleared again. Herculaneum was buried under a 20 m/65 ft high lava sludge layer and Pompeii was covered in 7 m/23 ft of ash and pumice. The death toll can only be an estimation but it is believed to be around 2000. The very volcano that had made the landscape so lush and fertile, providing such fruitful fields and vineyards, had turned the area into a desert. Ancient Stabiae, where the Sorrento Peninsula begins, was also wiped out, as well as the villa complex of Oplontis further afield. Mount Vesuvius and the Phlegraean Fields are under constant observation to this day. However, even with the advanced research abilities, neither earthquakes nor volcanic eruptions can be predicted with certainty. The European Civil Protection Mechanism also studies the eruption of AD 79 as the event provides illustrative material of the consequences of a volcanic eruption and offers insights in civil protection planning. Please note that the numbers on the maps on pages 50 and 54 are only for identifying the houses; they do not coincide with the numbers on site. *3 day combined ticket for Pompeii, Herculaneum, Villa Oplontis, Stabia, Boscoreale 22 euros, EU citizens under 18 free entry, 18–25 years 12 euros*

ERCOLANO (HERCULANEUM)

(134 B3) *(ⓜ D4)* ★ At the time of the eruption about 5000 people lived in Herculaneum, which was less of a busy industrial centre as Pompeii was, and far more of a neat, patrician residential area.

The 20 m/65 ft high lava sludge, found its way into every house, into every crack, and turned the city into stone and cement, in the process perfectly preserving it. It is better preserved than Pompeii: here you can even see furniture, roof beams, doors (see house no. 8 with a sliding door) and timber that has lasted for centuries. Today however, the site has a huge problem –

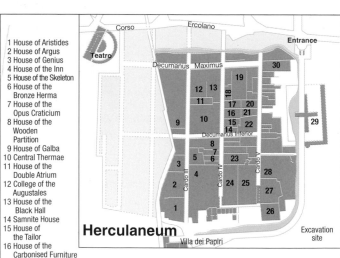

1 House of Aristides
2 House of Argus
3 House of Genius
4 House of the Inn
5 House of the Skeleton
6 House of the Bronze Herma
7 House of the Opus Craticium
8 House of the Wooden Partition
9 House of Galba
10 Central Thermae
11 House of the Double Atrium
12 College of the Augustales
13 House of the Black Hall
14 Samnite House
15 House of the Tailor
16 House of the Carbonised Furniture
17 House of the Neptune Mosaic
18 House of the Beautiful Courtyard
19 House of the Bicentenary
20 House of the Corinthian Atrium
21 House of the Wooden Sacellum
22 House of the Great Portal
23 House of the Alcove
24 House of the Mosaic Atrium
25 House of the Deer
26 Suburban Thermae
27 House of the Gem
28 House of the Relief of Telephus
29 Palaestra
30 Aula superiore

The ancient Herculaneum below the present-day town of Ercolano

the excavations have exposed the materials to oxygen and the elements and decay has set in. With modern methods and good common sense – hawks as pigeon control, restoration of the ancient sewerage system – the *Herculaneum Conservation Project (www.herculaneum. org)* has successfully managed to put a stop to the insidious destruction.

Over the centuries the city remained locked in lava and was forgotten, and became the site on which the town of *Resina*, today *Ercolano*, developed in the Middle Ages. After the first informal excavation attempts (under the Bourbon King Charles III), in 1827 layers of stone were lifted and entire houses were excavated, but it was only 100 years later that further work was conducted in a more scientific manner. In order to do so the houses above the ancient city had to be destroyed, which the inhabitants resisted (and continue to do so) because at least one third of the ancient city still serves as the foundation of the new.

Unlike Pompeii, which stretches out on a flat surface outside of the new settle-

The lava sludge perfectly preserved Herculaneum's mosaics just as they were two thousand years ago

ment, the ancient Herculaneum lies beneath the present-day Ercolano, where the half-demolished houses above act like a second layer of ruins. From the long, ramp-like ↘ avenue which leads down into the ancient city, you get a good overview.

SIGHTSEEING

EXCAVATIONS

A street grid runs through the old city ruins, consisting of three narrow lanes, which run from south to north, called Cardo III, IV and V on the map, they are crossed by two broad main streets, the *Decumanus Maximus* and the *Decumanus Inferior*. Along these bumpy cobbled streets are several dozen houses. One of these expensive residential buildings is the lavish villa complex *Casa dei Cervi* (House of Deer on Cardo V, map no. 25). On the southern side of the Cardo V are the *Terme Suburbane* (map no. 26), particularly interesting due to their thermal facilities, frescos and floor mosaics. On Cardo IV are a few houses where some wooden furniture has miraculously been preserved, *House no. 8* has a partition wall made from wood and *House no. 16* has charred furniture.

The *Villa dei Papiri,* another highlight of the excavatons, is cosed until further notice. But its elegant sculptures can be viewed at the National Museum in Naples and its Greek papyrus scrolls that were found here in 1800 in the National Library in Naples. *Daily 8.30am–5pm, April–Oct until 7.30pm | 11 euros | Corso Resina | www.pompeiisites.org (also online tickets)*

FOOD & DRINK

VIVA LO RE ⊘

Fine Slow Food *osteria* in an annexe of Villa Campolieto, also with some stylish guest rooms. *Closed Sun evening and Mon | Corso Resina 261 | tel. 08 17 39 02 07 | www.vivalore.it | Moderate*

WHERE TO STAY

INSIDER TIP FABRIC HOSTEL & CLUB

This is a great example of the new generation of "hostels" on the Gulf of Naples: high standards, small dorms (and also double rooms), restaurant, cool music club and no age limit. In an old weaving mill in the neighbouring municipality of Portici, a 10 minute walk from the Circumvesuviana Station Portici Via Libertà. *80 beds in 20 rooms | Via Bellucci Sessa 22 | tel. 08 17 76 58 74 | www.fabrichostel. com | Budget*

POMPEI (POMPEII)

(134 C4) (ꙮ E5) Pompeii is a hugely popular tourist attraction, but the ancient city is vast and is still reasonably empty in the early hours of the morning.

At the time Pompeii was buried under ash and pumice in AD 79 it was already an old, established town. The people of Pompeii produced and traded wine, oil, olives, wheat, fabric, wool, bricks and much more. Today's Pompeii (pop. 25,000) became – at the time of the first excavations – an important religious site when the *Santuario della Madonna del Rosario (www.santuario.it)* church from 1876 on the large piazza, became famous for a miracle, turning it into a pilgrimage destination that draws more than 4 million people each year (impressive communal prayers on 8 May and on first Sunday in October).

SIGHTSEEING

EXCAVATIONS

You enter the ruined city through the *Porta Marina* but before then a visit to the *Terme Suburbane* – outside the city walls – is a must. The luxurious public bathing facilities even had its own jetty, the interior walls are covered in refined stucco decorations, and the changing room walls have erotic illustrations which are believed to help bathers remember which boxes or lockers were theirs. Then you reach the area with the public buildings and squares: the *Temple of Venus* and *Apollo*, the large, three-aisled *Basilica*, the meeting room and the seat of the court as well as the extensive *Forum*, where the temples and markets are situated.

Further on is the *Via dell'Abbondanza* and the main shopping street, *Decumanus Maximus*, with its homes and shops and with the large public baths *Terme Stabiane* (there are two more baths), that face a small alley that leads to the left, to the *lupanare* (brothels). On the right of the main street there's the theatre district with a small and large *theatre*, the *gladiator barracks* and the *Temple of Isis*, whose marvellous, almost intact frescos can now be seen in the National Museum of Naples. The Via dell'Abbondanza leads to the other end of the town, the *Porta di Sarno*, past the wool cleaning and dyeing area, *Stephani*, to the large sports fields, the *palaestra* and to the huge 20,000 seater *amphitheatre*.

In front of the sporting ground you turn right to the town's ancient vineyards, some of which have been replanted. In one of the gardens, the **INSIDER TIP** *orto dei fuggiaschi*, you will encounter a glass case which contains the touching casts of the men, women and children who died whilst trying to escape the ash rain.

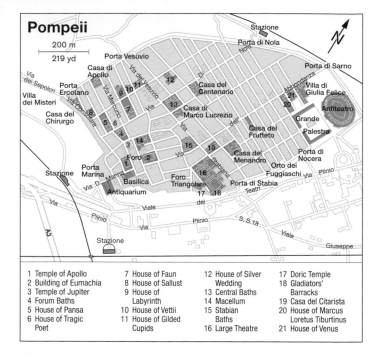

Pompeii

200 m
219 yd

Legend

1 Temple of Apollo
2 Building of Eumachia
3 Temple of Jupiter
4 Forum Baths
5 House of Pansa
6 House of Tragic Poet
7 House of Faun
8 House of Sallust
9 House of Labyrinth
10 House of Vettii
11 House of Gilded Cupids
12 House of Silver Wedding
13 Central Baths
14 Macellum
15 Stabian Baths
16 Large Theatre
17 Doric Temple
18 Gladiators' Barracks
19 Casa del Citarista
20 House of Marcus Loretus Tiburtinus
21 House of Venus

In the south-western part of the town there are the largest number of splendid private villas, most notably the large *Casa del Fauno* (the original statue of the dancing faun is in the Museum of Naples) and the *Casa dei Vettii*. The restored **INSIDER TIP** *House of Marco Lucrezio Fronton* is well worth seeing, especially the ochre yellow room containing frescoes of miniature landscapes and poignant portraits of children presumably depicting the children of the former owner.

A stroll along the walls around Pompeii, the **INSIDER TIP** *Passeggiata fuori le Mura* will give you a fantastic view of the ruined city. An absolute must-see is the ★ *Villa dei Misteri* just outside of the area, in the south-west. The beautiful 2nd century villa in the countryside has not revealed all its secrets: what are the people – especially the women – in the frescos doing, why does everyone in these wonderful frescos on the villa's interior appear so tense or is it so melancholic? There are numerous interpretations but the common belief is that the frescos depict a Dionysian initiation rite.

To preserve the mosaics on the floor and the frescos, not all rooms are accessible. The helpful audio guides and free maps with explanations are available at the entrance of Piazza Porta Marina. You can find maps of all the archaeological sites to download and a list of buildings with their opening times at *www.pompeiisites.org. Daily 8.30am–5pm, April–Oct until 7.30pm | 13 euros | www.pompeiisites.org (also online tickets)*

FOOD & DRINK

GARUM

Excellent restaurant named after the fermented fish sauce popular in Pompeii times. It is advisable to reserve a table! *Closed Sun evening and Wed | Via Mazzini 63 | tel. 08 18 50 11 78 | www.ristoran tegarumpompei.it | Budget–Moderate*

IL PRINCIPE

Cuisine inspired by the ancient Roman world, in the centre of modern Pompeii. Delicious snacks in the wine bar. *In winter closed Sun and Mon evenings | Piazza Bartolo Longo 8 | tel. 08 18 50 55 66 | www. ilprincipe.com | Expensive*

WHERE TO STAY

HOTEL FORUM

35 beautiful rooms very near to the excavations. *Via Roma 99 | tel. 08 18 50 11 70 | www.hotelforum.it | Budget–Moderate*

INFORMATION

Via Sacra 1 and Piazza Porta Marina Inferiore 11 | tel. 08 18 57 53 47 | www. pompeiisites.org, www.pompeiturismo. it

WHERE TO GO

BOSCOREALE

(134 C3–4) *(*∅ *E4–5)*

Known for its **INSIDER TIP** *antiquarium* with interesting findings and reconstructions of ancient agriculture, as well as the ruins of a Roman estate, about 3 km/ 1.8 mile from Pompeii. *Daily 8.30am– 6pm, April–Oct until 7.30pm | combination ticket for Oplontis, Stabia, Boscoreale 5.50 euros | Via Settetermini 15*

CASTELLAMMARE DI STABIA

(134 C4) *(*∅ *E5)*

The small town 6 km/3.7 miles away, a thermal resort in ancient times, was

Villa dei Misteri: the mysterious secrets of melancholic young women

VESUVIO (VESUVIUS)

Steep hike up lava gravel to look down into the crater

(134 C3) (⊞ E4) This dangerous 12,000 year old (young) volcano is not only responsible for devastating towns such as Pompeii, Herculaneum and Stabiae (in AD 79) – a later eruption (in 1631) once again destroyed many of its surrounding villages and claimed an estimated 4000 lives.

The eruptions of 1906 and 1944 were also devastating. The volcano is still active today, although it seldom emits any smoke, under the 3 km/1.8 mile plug of hardened lava that clogs up the mouth, seethes magma at a depth of 5–7 km/3–4 miles. The split into two peaks, the former Monte Somma and the new crater (1281 m/4200 ft), happened during the eruption of AD 79. Despite the danger the immediate surroundings around Mount Vesuvius are still densely populated, this is due to the fact that the volcano has made the soil extremely fertile. Around 700,000 people live in the 18 communities at the foot of the volcano.

The most convenient way to get to the ☼ crater is to take the road from Ercolano that ends in a car park, from here it is another 30 minute walk across lava fields, you may want to use walking sticks (which you can rent) to help you on this stretch. At the summit are souvenir shops and the ticket office, because you can only access the rim of the crater if you pay a fee *(10 euros). Guided tours daily 9am–2 hrs before sunset | www.vesuviopark.it*

Once on the rim you will be able see down into the crater where there are a few isolated vents with plumes of steam. The view from the crater is overwhelming

built over the ruins of ancient Stabiae and is today surrounded by concrete buildings. A ☼ hike *(Passeggiata Archeologica)* above the town leads to the ruins of two beautifully situated Roman patrician villas. *Daily 8.30am–5pm, April–Oct until 7.30pm | combination ticket for Oplontis, Stabia, Boscoreale 5.50 euros*

but the climb is only advisable when the weather is calm and there's a clear view. Mount Vesuvius is now a national park (*www.parconazionaledelvesuvio.it*) with 50 km/31 miles of signposted hiking trails. The seismological observation centre, *Osservatorio Storico Vesuviano* from 1841 *(closed at the moment due to restorations | www.ov.ingv.it)* is on the road from Herculaneum to Mount Vesuvius and has an exhibition about the history of the volcano.

VILLA OPLONTIS ★
(134 C4) (*∅ E5*)
In the middle of *Torre Annunziata,* one of those rather shabby towns along the Gulf coast lies what is probably the most beautiful villa of the Roman period – buried by Vesuvius's AD 79 eruption. One must imagine that this beautiful country estate with its brightly painted rooms, courtyards, baths, pools and gardens was once in the middle of a lush, green landscape overlooking the sea. So far nearly two-thirds of the estate has been excavated. This grandiose and well-preserved villa – it is said to have once belonged to Poppea, Nero's wife – is rarely visited by tourists, making a visit a special experience. *Daily 8.30am–5pm, April–Oct until 7.30pm | combination ticket for Oplontis, Stabia, Boscoreale 5.50 euros | Via dei Sepolcri*

VILLE VESUVIANE
(134 B3) (*∅ D4*)
What the Roman patricians enjoyed doing, so did the aristocracy of the Kingdom of Naples in the 18th century: they liked to build themselves luxurious country villas in the lovely countryside with views on to the Gulf and the spectacularly smouldering volcano. Charles III had his country home, *Palazzo Reale,* built here in *Portici* in 1738 with large parks and hunting grounds. Hundreds of villas were built between Portici and Herculaneum and the stretch was called the *Miglio d'Oro* but one can no longer talk of the "golden mile" these days.

About 120 villas remain, neglected and hemmed in by modern, shabby housing developments. You can view some of them, such as the exemplary restored ★ ≋ *Villa Campolieto (Corso Resina 283)* in Herculaneum. The elegant, elliptical belvedere portico was designed by star architect Luigi Vanvitelli. You can also visit the two nearby villas, *Villa Petti Ruggiero (Via Alessandro Rossi 42)* and *Villa Favorita (Via Gabriele D'Annunzio 36): all Tue–Sun 10am–1pm.* In July concerts and dances are performed in the villas. *www.villevesuviane.net*

CAPRI, ISCHIA, PROCIDA

Each of the three islands in the Gulf is a world of its own; each draws its own unique set of visitors. In the summer and on weekends thousands of day trippers swarm in, especially to Capri.

Travel on the islands is on foot, by bus and on Ischia and Procida with small, rattling three-wheeled taxis, while on Capri electric carts whirr through the streets.

CAPRI

(134 A6) (*C–D 6–7*) ★ The island is a 4 mile² limestone rock off the outermost tip of the Sorrento Peninsula.

Two of the island's towns are on high plateaus, the capital *Capri* with its winding white alleys, fine boutiques, elegant hotels and the Marina Grande harbour, where the ferries dock, and Marina Piccola, the picturesque bay on the southern side; the second is *Anacapri,* larger and more spread out, quieter and not as sophisticated. The island was discovered by the Roman Emperor Augustus. Emperor Tiberius spent 14 years on the island, enchanted by the flower maquis, the beautiful views, the bizarre rock formations as well as the *Faraglioni* and the *Arco Naturale,* but also by the many grottoes, among them the *Grotta Azzurra,* the Blue Grotto.

SIGHTSEEING

ANACAPRI
In the village of Anacapri (pop. 6700) make a stop at the ★ *San Michele* church

Sophisticated life on Capri's Piazzetta, curative thermal springs on Ischia, idyll under fragrant lemon groves on Procida

(April–Sept daily 9am–7pm, Oct–March 10am–3pm | www.chiesa-san-michele. com) with its wonderful majolica floor, where the expulsion of Adam and Eve from the Garden of Eden is depicted in colourful detail. There is also the perfectly positioned 1896 summer home ⚡ *Villa San Michele (May–Sept daily 9am–6pm, March, April and Oct 9am–5pm, Nov–Feb 9am–3.30pm | Via Capodimonte | www.san michele.eu)* belonging to the Swedish doctor and writer Axel Munthe. A lane leads from the Piazza Vittoriato the villa.

Various paths lead up ⚡ *Monte Solaro* (589 m/1932 ft) but it is also accessible by chairlift. This is also where you will find the medieval hermitage and pilgrimage church the **INSIDER TIP** *Santa Maria a Cetrella*, with Madonna shrine, as well as the viewing terrace ⚡ *Belvedere della Migliara* overlooking the steep rocky coast. For some tasty country cuisine, five beautiful rooms and a swimming pool (also for day guests), try *Da Gelsomina alla Migliara (April–Dec daily | tel. 08 18 37 14 99 | www.dagelsomina.com | Expensive).*

Giardini di Augusto terrace gardens with panoramic views in all directions

You can swim and enjoy a delicious meal for example at the *Lido del Faro* beach club *(www.lidofaro.com)* nestled in a rocky cove at the lighthouse at the *Punta Carena,* the south-west tip (on foot or by shuttle bus). Across from there is the legendary *Marina Piccola* (which, thanks to its south facing location, is sunnier than Marina Grande) which has some exclusive bathing lidos (e.g. the renowned La Fontelina) on a few spots of beach and rocky slabs.

CAPRI

From the harbour town of *Marina Grande* – with its piers for the ferries, excursion boats and yachts, a few cafés, restaurants and a narrow strip of sandy beach – you can walk via a stepped path into the heart of Capri (pop. 7000) or you can take the quicker route up by cable car (there is a left luggage storage for day trippers).

The centre of town is the famous *Piazzetta* (Piazza Umberto I) full of attractive (and expensive) cafés. During the day, the place is crowded with day trippers but in the evenings it becomes a charming meeting place for permanent guests, the jet-set and the locals. The picturesque town is the perfect mixture of a maze of alleys and elegant hotels, restaurants and shops. Shopping tip: the fine perfumes by *Carthusia – Profuni di Capri (Viale Parco Augusto 2 | www.carthusia. it),* an old fragrance company.

One of the sightseeing attractions is the *Carthusian Monastery of San Giacomo*, an impressive 14th century monastery complex, which is now used for cultural events. The monastery, which got its present-day appearance the 16th century, is built on the remains of one of the twelve villas of Emperor Tiberius. There is a permanent exhibition in the refectory *(Tue–Sun 9am–2pm and 5pm–8pm | Via Certosa | www.capricertosa.com)* with enormous paintings by Karl Wilhelm Diefenbach who lived on the island from 1899 until his death in 1913. There are stunning panoramic views from the ☆ *Giardini di Augusto* and the gardens are also where the famous, steep serpentine cliff path, the ☆ *Via Krupp* begins. The German industrialist, Alfred Krupp, had the switchback foot path carved into the cliff in 1902 and it snakes down to the popular *Marina Piccola* swimming bay, however it is sometimes closed due to danger of falling rocks (information on closures: *tel. 08 18 37 06 86*). Here the three *Faraglioni* rock boulders rise from the sea, Capri's famous landmark.

Of the twelve villas on Capri built by Emperor Tiberius in AD 27–37 (when he ruled the Roman Empire from here) the ☆ *Villa Jovis (Wed–Mon 9am–2pm | on the eastern tip, signposted)* is the most magnificent. The remains of the villa include most of its walls, cisterns and thermal baths. A walk (45 min) leads through the lush villa gardens to the beautifully exposed ruins.

The quickest way to escape Capri's day trippers is on foot, and at the same time you will get to know the most beautiful corners of the island. Simply follow the blue ceramic signs, such as the one from *La Croce* to the west on the *Via Matermania* in the direction of the *Arco Naturale*. The loop route leads along the wild south coast past the restaurant Le Grottelle, past the *Grotta di Matermania* and above the spectacularly situated *Villa Malaparte* back to the panoramic *Belvedere di Tragara* lookout point.

GROTTA AZZURRA

The Blue Grotto, with its dazzling play of sunlight on brilliant blue water, is probably the most famous grotto in the world. You can reach it from Marina Grande *(boat trip incl. entrance fee 29 euros)* or from Anacapri. The walk from Anacapri takes about 45 minutes, you can also take the public bus and there are excursion boats at the pier *(then incl. entrance about 13 euros). Daily 9am–sunset, rough seas mean that it is not always accessible*

FOOD & DRINK

BUONOCORE ● ☺

The specialty of this celebrated ice cream parlour is their "Fantasia di Capri". *Closed Tue | Via Vittorio Emanuele 35*

LA CAPANNINA

Elegant, family-run restaurant in the centre. Local cuisine and excellent wines (also available to take away in the delicatessen next door). *April–Oct daily | Via Le Botteghe 12 | tel. 08 18 37 07 32 | www.capanninacapri.com | Moderate–Expensive*

LIDO DEL FARO ●

Beach club at Punta Carena near the Anacapri lighthouse: lido, restaurant, bar and lounge rolled into one – this is where the locals go swimming. *April–Mid Oct.*

⭐ **Capri**
The small island with the world-famous Blue Grotto is also a hiker's paradise → p. 58

⭐ **San Michele**
Capri's beautiful hand painted majolica tile floor → p. 58

⭐ **La Mortella**
Exotic Mediterranean garden paradise on Ischia → p. 63

⭐ **Negombo**
Thermal spa with a meditative Zen-like atmosphere, in a beautiful bay on Ischia → p. 64

MARCO POLO HIGHLI...

*daily | tel. 08 18 37 17 98 | www.
lidofaro.com | Moderate*

LO SFIZIO
Unpretentious family *trattoria* on the way
to Villa Jovis, recommended by the locals.
In the evenings they also serve pizza. *Except
July/Aug closed Tue | Via Tiberio 7e | tel.
08 18 37 41 28 | www.losfiziocapri.com |
Budget–Moderate*

WHERE TO STAY

HOTEL VILLA BRUNELLA ﹅
This charmingly elegant hotel is on a series
of terraces with swimming pool, excellent
restaurant and nice views of Marina Picola.
*20 rooms | Via Tragara 24 | tel. 08 18 37 01 22 |
www.villabrunella.it | Expensive*

VILLA SARAH
Charming family hotel with pool. 15 min-
ute walk to the centre of Capri. *19 rooms |
Via Tiberio 3 | tel. 08 18 37 78 17 | www.
villasarahcapri.com | Moderate–Expensive*

INFORMATION

*At Marina Grande harbour | tel. 08 18
37 06 34; Capri: Piazzetta | tel. 08 18 37
06 86; Anacapri: Via Orlandi 59 | tel. 08 18
37 15 24; www.capritourism.com, www.
capri.net*

ISCHIA

(132 A–B6) (𝄞 A–B5) **Ischia (pop.
62,000, 17 miles²) is the largest of the
Gulf islands and together with Procida
lies at the northern arc of the Gulf of
Naples.**

he island owes its fame to its volcanic
ture: it has an extinct volcano, Mount
meo and craters (also underwater
s), 103 hot springs, 69 fumarole fields

and volcanic mud – making it a major
draw card for tourists. The island was also
popular with the Romans who came here
for thermal treatments. Today it has over
400 hotels catering to 3.4 million tourists
who come annually for spa treatments.
Aside from its beaches and thermal treatments, Ischia also offers many hiking
trails, such as the hike from Fontana up
﹅ *Epomeo* (788 m/2585 ft).

SIGHTSEEING

NORTH COAST
The island's capital, Ischia, lies in the
northeast and has two different centres,
picturesque *Ischia Ponte* and *Ischia Porto,*
the harbour quarter, with a lively entertainment mile, the so-called Rive Droite.
Here you'll find a restaurant popular with
the young crowd, the *L'Altra Mezzanotte
(daily in the summer | Via Porto 71 | tel.
0 81 98 17 11 | Budget–Moderate).* Ischia
Ponte (*ponte* = bridge) has a footbridge
that connects it with the *Castello
Aragonese (daily 9am–1 hr before sunset |
www.castelloaragonese.it)* built on a rock
island. It has twelve churches and a monastery that has been converted into a
simple yet stylish hotel: ﹅ *Il Monastero
(21 rooms | tel. 0 81 99 24 35 | www.albergo
ilmonastero.it | Moderate).* A number of
thermal springs are spread out along the
north coast, and it is greener than in the
steeper, hotter south.
Casamicciola is a relatively modern town.
Having the most thermal springs, it is the
main destination for tourists on spa pack-
age tours. The historic *Manzi Therme* re-
opened as a luxurious Albergo with the
*Ristorante Il Mosaico (Piazza Bagni 4 | tel.
08 1 99 47 22 | www.termemanzihotel.
com | Expensive)* where a Michelin star
chef from Ischia does his magic. For all his
culinary artistry, chef Nino Di Costanzo
remains true to local traditions. The re-

sort town of *Lacco Ameno* also has some exclusive villas and luxurious hotels, such as the *Mezzatorre Resort & Spa* luxury hotel *(57 rooms | Via Mezzatorre 23 | tel. 0 81 98 61 11 | www.mezzatorre.it | Expensive)* set in a pine grove, on the high cape west of Lacco Ameno, above the beautiful bay Baia di San Montano.

SOUTH COAST

The quaint, former fishing village of *Sant'Angelo* is another popular destination. Its simple white and pastel-coloured hous-

The municipality of *Barano* is the centre of Ischia's culinary traditions, with its vineyards and the popular local speciality, a particularly tasty wild rabbit stew, the best (Slow Food!) of which is served at ⊙ *Il Focolare (June–Oct closed Mon evening, Tue evening, Wed evening, Nov–mid May closed Wed | Via Cretajo al Crocefisso 3 | tel. 0 81 90 29 44 | Budget–Moderate).*

WEST COAST

Forio was an artist's enclave during the 1950s and in the lively, old town centre you

Popular destination: the picturesque fishing village of Sant' Angelo

es hug the hillside and are crisscrossed by narrow alleys and stairs that lead down to the sea. In the foreground is the small, wooded peninsula of *Punta Sant´Angelo* with its castle ruin. Sant'Angelo also has a lovely sandy beach ● *Spiaggia dei Maronti* where the underground volcanic activity heats up the dark sand. The beautiful and modern*San Giorgio (65 rooms | tel. 0 81 99 00 98 | www.hotelsangiorgio.com | Moderate–Expensive)* hotel resort is also located here.

can find the picturesque little *Santa Maria del Soccorso* church, numerous hotels and two beautiful, sandy beaches: *Spiaggia di Citara* and *Spiaggia di San Francesco*. A small refuge in a fantastic location is **INSIDER TIP** *Il Poggio Antico (4 rooms, 4 flats | Via Bellomo 2 | tel. 0 81 98 61 23 | www.ilpoggioantico.com | Moderate)* with thermal water pool. Near Forio is the enchanting ★ ☆ *La Mortella (April–Oct Tue, Thu, Sat, Sun 9am–7pm | Via Francesco Calise 39 | www.lamortella.org),* a sub-

Hot baths guarantee relaxation: thermal spa Giardini di Poseidon

tropical and Mediterranean garden with a teahouse and concert programme.

THERMAL SPAS

The thermal spa in Sant'Angelo is *Aphrodite Apollo (tel. 0 81 99 92 19 | www. hotelmiramaresearesort.it)*, the *Parco Castiglione (SS 270 at Punta la Scrofa | tel. 0 81 98 25 51 | www.termecastiglione. it)* in Casamicciola is quite expensive (and very German) while the *Giardini di Poseidon (tel. 08 19 08 71 11 | www.giar diniposeidonterme.com)* at Forio's Citara beach lives up to its name and is a real garden oasis. In the centre of Ischia Porto is the modern *Terme di Ischia (Via delle Terme 15 | tel. 0 81 98 54 89 | www.ter meischia.eu)* open throughout the year. Tucked into the picturesque bay of San Montano, and surrounded by maquis and rocky cliffs, is the wonderful ther-mal park ★ *Negombo (tel. 0 81 98 61 52 | www.negombo.it)* at Lacco Ameno with

a very good INSIDER TIP terrace restau-rant *(Moderate)*. The thermal parks are generally open from April to October, day entrance fee: 25–30 euros.

INFORMATION

Porto d'Ischia | Via Iasolino 7 | tel. 08 15 07 42 31 | www.ischiaonline.it, www. infoischiaprocida.it, www.pithecusa.com

PROCIDA

(132 B5–6) (ØØ B5) **When you take the hydrofoil to scenic Procida it will only take you 35 minutes to leave the busy chaos of Naples for the peace and calm of the island.**

The island may be small (1.5 mile²) but with a population of a good 10,000 it is quite densely populated. Like Ischia it is of volcanic in origin with lots of bays and a jagged coastline and its fertile volcanic soil produces flourishing lemon and orange groves. The Neapolitans love Procida, it is just the right size, easily accessible and relatively inexpensive: the perfect Mediterranean island for a family retreat. Ferries run several times a day between Pozzuoli, Naples and Ischia.

SIGHTSEEING

ISLAND ROUNDTRIP

The old town, *Terra Murata*, lies on the highest point (90 m/297 ft) of the island. From the harbour – with its fishermen's houses, restaurants, cafés and the waiting three-wheeled mini taxis – it only takes a few minutes to get up to the ✹ *Palazzo Baronale* fortress on a steep cliff. From here you can enjoy a magnificent view of the Gulf and the island with its light-coloured houses set in lush, green citrus gardens. At the foot of the mountain lies the fishing village of INSIDER TIP *Corricella*, its colourful little houses and blue boats make it the most picturesque corner of Procida.

Another harbour village, *Chiaiolella,* lies at the other end of the island on a small inlet and this is where most of the activity takes place: beaches, lots of hotels and the outlying little island of *Vivara,* a forest and bird paradise.

FOOD & DRINK

CARACALÈ

Enjoy delicious fresh fish right on the harbour jetty in Corricella. *Closed Tue, closed in winter Mon–Fri | Marina Corricella | tel. 08 18 96 91 92 | Moderate*

LO SCARABEO

Relax on the lemon tree terrace in Ciraccio and tuck into the local rabbit dish. *In winter closed Mon | Via Salette 10 | tel. 08 18 96 99 18 | Budget*

WHERE TO STAY

LA CASA SUL MARE ✹

Below the castle, with ten bright rooms (with balcony) and fantastic views. *Salita Castello 13 | tel. 08 18 96 87 99 | www.la casasulmare.it | Moderate*

HOTEL RISTORANTE CRESCENZO

Good cuisine and open throughout the year. A few of the ✹ rooms have sea views and the beach is just a walk away. *10 rooms | Marina Chiaiolella 33 | tel. 08 18 96 72 55 | www.hotelcrescenzo.it | Moderate*

INFORMATION

Via Roma 109 | tel. 08 18 96 80 89 | www. infoischiaprocida.it | www.procida.net

LOW BUDGET

The hour-long (approx.) ferry crossing from Pozzuoli to Procida is a mini-cruise with a reasonable price tag *(one-way 9.70 euros | www.care mar.it).* It goes across the Gulf of Pozzuoli and past the Capo Miseno.

The ruins of ✹ *Villa Damecuta* on Capri, where the Roman Emperor Tiberius spent his summer, can be viewed free of charge and its magnificent panoramic view is also free!

Free thermal bath: at Ischia Ponte's *Carta Romana* beach, at the ● sandy bay of *Sorgeto* near Panza and near Sant'Angelo at the beaches of *Cava Grande* and *Maronti*. These are all places where fumaroles rise up from the sand, or hot springs mingle with the seawater.

THE AMALFI COAST

It is called the _Costa Divina_, the divine coast and it begins in the foothills of the Monti Lattari, which jut into the sea as a peninsula and form the southern arc of the Gulf of Naples.

This is where the town of Sorrento is perched high above the sea. In addition to beautiful hotels the Sorrento Peninsula also offers some of the best gourmet restaurants in southern Italy, with panoramic views of Mount Vesuvius and Naples. At the extreme tip of the Sorrento Peninsula is the Punta Campanella nature reserve with its strictly protected flora and fauna and pretty Capri is within arm's reach. Further east the Amalfitana starts – the narrow, winding, 40 km/25 miles long scenic road that runs along the cliff coast – with stunning views of the cobalt-blue sea, fragrant lemon groves, and picture-perfect villages that cling to the ravines and cliffs.

From Easter through to autumn there is daily traffic (and parking space) chaos, especially at weekends. During the day no private buses, camper vans and caravans are allowed on this road in summer. So the best option is for you to either take the bus, or come across on one of the regular ferries from Naples, Sorrento, Salerno, the Cilento coast and the islands.

Located high above the rocky coast, Ravello is for many Italy's most beautiful belvedere. And from the ceramics town of Vietri sul Mare the view is of the Gulf of Salermo and the old, bustling port town.

A Mediterranean dream: hiking on old mule paths through lemon groves high above the picturesque, pastel-coloured towns

AMALFI

(135 D5) (*∅ F6*) **Amalfi is made up of a jumble of white houses, two squares and a main street – all connected by lots of quaint, winding alleys and stairs. There are also seven churches, a magnificent cathedral, the harbour, and the labyrinth-like narrow, medieval passageway, Rua Nova Mercatorum, that goes on and on through the maze of houses in an almost oriental manner.**

All of this is crammed in between the sea and the dramatic Valle dei Mulini (valley of mills) ravine, which goes up the rocky shore like a steep-sided funnel. At least 5200 people live on this narrow space.

In the Middle Ages, when Amalfi was one of four great maritime Republics (Pisa, Genoa, Venice) – that controlled the movement of goods between the Orient and Occident with their merchant fleets – it was said to be over 50,000. That was until the city was forced to its knees in

Vertiginous houses tumbling down the cliff in a cascade to the small beach at Amalfi

1135 by rival Pisa and landslides and storm surges plunged part of it into the sea. The region became marginalised and turned instead to fishing, handiwork, jewellery making and – more importantly – to the precious production of paper (learnt from the Arabs) with up to 16 paper mills working the valley's powerful mountain streams.

This all changed with the construction of the coastal road in 1832 and the arrival of the first foreigners, artists, and writers. Amalfi's two large monasteries, both from the 13th century, were converted into magnificent hotels: the Luna and the Cappuccini. And Amalfi became the place where the sensitive and wealthy from the north could sit out the winter, from October through to March. And today? The confines of its location means that it is unlikely that Amalfi's development will spiral out of control, it does get plenty of visitors but despite its popularity the city has kept its charm and remains the (expensive) backdrop for the good life, for good food (expensive) and for the wonderful spectacle of nature from dawn to dusk.

SIGHTSEEING

ARSENALE

The impressive brick building was once part of the medieval shipyards, today it hosts exhibitions, it is just off the *Piazza Flavio Gioia* (named after the inventor of the compass).

DUOMO SANT'ANDREA/ CHIOSTRO DEL PARADISO

At the top of a wide, sweeping staircase is the town's impressive cathedral. The façade has black and white marble stone and open arches with gables colourfully tiled in mosaics. A landslide collapsed part of the church in 1861 but it was faithfully rebuilt. Only the church tower (1180) with its majolica tiled minaret domes remained standing, but even before the collapse the cathedral had been remodelled several times and the broad, pillared arcade façade hides two churches and a cloister with a melange of style elements that include Arab, Norman and baroque. The original church is the 10th century *Cappella del Crocifisso*, now free of its baroque stucco and, since 1995, an attractive *cathedral museum*. The three-aisled main church dates back to the 11th century, when the marine Republic was at the height of its wealth and power. It has a *bronze portal* from Constantinople, a masterpiece of oriental art that dates back to 1066. There is also the baroque-designed crypt with the reliquary of St Andrew, the first Apostle, who is highly venerated in Amalfi as a patron saint. The cloister, which has an oriental look and feel with its dual arches, ★ *Chiostro del Paradiso*, from the 13th century was once the burial place for Amalfi's aristocracy. *Chiostro del Paradiso and Museo del*

Duomo May–Sept daily 9am–9pm, Oct and Jan–April 9am–7pm, Nov/Dec 10am–5pm

MUSEO DELLA BUSSOLA
If you are interested in Amalfi's history as a naval power, you should look at the historic document, the *Tabula Amalphitana*, the Republic's medieval maritime and commercial code. *Tue–Sun 10am–1pm and 4pm–7pm | Largo Cesareo Console 3/Piazza Flavio Gioia*

MUSEO DELLA CARTA
The famous paper factories in Amalfi, which once supplied offices of the Kingdom of Naples, never made the transition to modernisation at the end of the 19th century and only two workshops have survived to the present-day. They offer the highest quality craftsmanship: INSIDER TIP *Amatruda* and *Antica Cartiera Amalfitana* in Tramonti. The paper is long-lasting, highly prized by artists and used for rare bibliophile treasures. The paper museum details the history of this tradi-

---

★ Chiostro del Paradiso
A touch of the Orient in the Sant'Andrea cathedral in Amalfi, burial place for Amalfi nobility
→ p. 69

★ Antichi Sentieri
Hike along the old mule paths surrounded by wonderful nature and breathtaking views → p. 70

★ Duomo San Pantaleone
Precious mosaics and a Byzantine bronze portal in Ravello's cathedral. Less known: an ampoule relic of the patron saint's blood liquefies here once a year, on 27 July → p. 76

★ Terrazza dell'Infinito
Ravello's viewing terrace has never-ending views over the coast and the sea and there is a delightful garden café below the terrace → p. 77

★ Duomo di Salerno
Salerno's Romanesque cathedral has oriental pillars, beautiful baroque décor, and an Apostle in the crypt → p. 78

★ Locanda Don Alfonso 1890
Campania's top restaurant is in Sant'Agata sui due Golfi, and the ingredients are supplied by their own organic farm → p. 83

MARCO POLO HIGHLIGHTS

tion. *March-Oct daily 10am–6.30pm, Nov–Feb Tue/Wed and Fri–Sun 10am–3.30pm | Via delle Cartiere 23 | www.museodellacarta.it*

FOOD & DRINK

DONNA STELLA

Fantastic pizzeria in a lemon tree garden. The deep-fried specialties are highly recommended. *Closed Mon | Salita Rascica 2 | tel. 33 83 58 84 83 | Budget–Moderate*

PANSA

A traditional café on the Piazza del Duomo, with delicious specialities from lemon cakes to *limoncello*, everything made using lemons from their own groves. Also tasty snacks. *Daily | www.pasticceriapansa.it | Budget–Moderate*

SHOPPING

Writing paper, notebooks, albums made of Amatruda paper as well as antique town maps and views of Amalfi are all available at *Antiche Stampe di Amalfi (Piazza Duomo 10)*.

BEACHES

There is a small sandy beach at Amalfi; otherwise you can retreat to the bays and jetties or the dark, sandy beaches of the neighbouring Atrani.

WHERE TO STAY

An affordable alternative to the expensive hotels are the holiday homes and B&Bs. *www.bed-and-breakfast.it, www.ercolediamalfi.it*

RESIDENZA LUCE

Small yet modern hotel full of local charm situated in the centre. *10 rooms | Salita Fra Gerardo Sasso 4 | tel. 0 89 87 15 37 | www.residenzaluce.it | Moderate*

LA PERGOLA ☆

Small hotel on the leafy outskirts of town (on the coastal road, in the suburb of Vettica) that also serves delicious cuisine at reasonable prices. *12 rooms | Via Augustaccio 10 | tel. 0 89 83 10 88 | www.lapergolamalfi.it | Budget–Moderate*

SANT'ANDREA

Nice guesthouse with a view on to the cathedral piazza. *9 rooms | Piazza Duomo | tel. 0 89 87 11 45 | www.albergosantandrea.it | Budget*

SANTA CATERINA ☆

Above the cliffs, Amalfi's most elegant (and most expensive) hotel with excellent restaurant. *69 rooms | Via Nazionale 9 | tel. 0 89 87 10 12 | www.hotelsantacaterina.it | Expensive*

INFORMATION

Corso Repubbliche Marinare 27 | tel. 0 89 87 11 07 | www.amalfitouristoffice.it

WHERE TO GO

ANTICHI SENTIERI (ANCIENT MOUNTAIN PATHS) ★ ☆ (135 D5) (𝄴 F6)

On the Amalfi Coast you will not want to lie on the beach the whole day: for many decades holiday guests have used the old mule paths and stairways behind Amalfi for hikes into the mountains, into a different world. The walks go along terraces of lemon and orange groves, through forests and ravines, on hills with small villages, such as *Pogerola* and *Pontone* with fantastic views of the coast.

A classic hike leads into the *Valle dei Mulini* with its ruins of old mills, waterfalls and dense forests, another goes through pretty Atrani up to Ravello. More challenging is a ⚞ mountain hike into the nature reserve *Valle delle Ferriere* full of rare plant species (especially ferns). The path has been signposted by the Italian Alpine Club (CAI) and goes up to 1000 m/3200 ft, into an alpine landscape, famous for its breathtaking views. The crowning is the famous ● *Sentiero degli Dei*, which begins in Bomerano, a suburb of Agerola. Bomerano is easy to get to by public bus *(www.sitabus.it)* from Amalfi. The well signposted path begins at the Piazza Capasso, where you can also shop for a picnic. It takes 3 hours to hike over the saddle of *Colle La Serra*, through villages such as *Nocelle* and *Montepertuso* and then finally down many steps to *Positano*. You can then return to Amalfi by either bus or boat *(www.coopsantandrea. it, www.travelmar.it, www.lucibello.it)*. Ask for maps at the tourist office or in Amalfi's newsagents, or visit *www. cartotrekking.com* and *www.giovis.com*.

EASTERN AMALFITANA
(135 D–E5) (*ん F–G6*)

Alongside Amalfi is INSIDER TIP ▶ *Atrani*, it is not as expensive but very picturesque with well-preserved white houses, winding stepped alleys and quaint squares such as the enchanting *Piazzetta Umberto I*. The *San Salvatore de Bireto* church has a beautiful oriental bronze portal from 1087. There a number of accommodation options including the small, pleasant *Ostello A'Scalinatella (12 rooms | Piazza Umberto I 5/6 | tel. 0 89 87 14 92 | www.hostel scalinatella.com | Budget)* at the centre and a few nice B&Bs *(www.larginefiorito. com | www.lascoglierarooms.com | Budget–Moderate)* and a row of inviting restaurants, e.g. the slow food place ⊗ *'a Paranza (daily in the summer, otherwise*

The Sentiero degli Dei high above the coast offering spectacular views of Positano

closed Tue | Via Dragone 1/2 | tel. 0 89 87 18 40 | Budget–Moderate).

Next up are *Minori* and *Maiori*, both situated on small estuaries, with wide sandy beaches, palm promenades and a more modern tourist infrastructure. In Minori there are also some impressive remains of a Roman villa.

At the ✹ *Capo d'Orso* (cape bear) are the remains of an 11th century Benedictine abbey and divine views of the Amalfi Coast and the Sorrento Peninsula all the way to Capri. It is followed by the small village of *Erchie*, situated deep in a valley gorge with a golden sandy bay. Next is the picturesque fishing village *Cetara* with its *San Pietro* church (majolica decorated dome) that is also the starting point of a beach procession on 29 June.

The end of the Amalfitana is at *Vietri sul Mare* (pop. 8300) a town with a proud ceramic heritage that dates back to the time of the Etruscans. It is lined with one shop after another full of colourfully glazed dishes, jugs and vases all stacked up against walls decorated with majolica tiles. In Raito is the *ceramics museum* which is housed in the *Torretta*, a tower set in the park and gardens that surround the *Villa Guariglia (June–mid Sept Tue–Sun 9am–7pm, mid Sept–May 9am–3pm)*. The *Ceramica Artistica Solimene (Via Madonna degli Angeli 7)* is one of the renovated ceramic factories in the town worth visiting for its spectacular majolica tiling.

WESTERN AMALFITANA
(134–135 C–D5) (𝄞 F6)

West of Amalfi is the picturesque village of *Conca dei Marini* where the road leads to the car park for the *Grotta dello Smeraldo (daily 10am–2.30pm, closed when the sea is rough, info: tel. 0 89 83 15 35)*, a magnificent refracted light limestone grotto with emerald-green water. The grotto measures 60 × 30 m/197 × 99 ft. High up

on a cliff above the coast lies the white monastery *Santa Rosa,* whose nuns invented the famous *sfogliatella* – pastries made with ricotta and candied fruits – celebrated here on the second weekend of August.

As your journey continues towards Positano, the coast road passes over the dramatic **INSIDER TIP** *Furore fjord* and the two hamlets of *Furore*. One high on the mountain between terraced vines (good local wine) and lemon groves, the other down on the coast, both connected by a long, stone staircase where goods were once carried from the ravine-like harbour bay up to the village. Every September during the **INSIDER TIP** *muri d'autore* artists come to transform the

house walls into artworks by painting them with colourful scenes. This and the dramatic natural scenery have made Furore *(www.furore.it)* a popular destination, evidenced by a number of small, charming hotels such as the pleasant *Locanda del Fiordo (11 rooms | Via Trasita 9 | tel. 0 89 87 48 13 | www.lalocandadel fiordo.it | Moderate)* and restaurant s like the *Hostaria di Bacco (daily | tel. 0 89 83 03 60 | www.baccofurore.it | Budget– Moderate)* with hotel *(19 rooms)* in the upper part of town.

Praiano – a village set between gardens and olive groves with a beautiful, majolica decorated church *San Gennaro* – and Vettica Maggiore are on the sunny ridge of Capo Sottile. Here lies the beautiful, small ☆ *Hotel Margherita (30 rooms | Via Umberto I 70 | tel. 0 89 87 46 28 | www.hotelmargherita.info | Budget– Moderate)* with seawater swimming pool and fantastic views. At the mouth of a ravine, between two sloping hillsides is *Marina di Praia* with its pebble beach and diving opportunities. The former fishing village is now a collection of guesthouses and pleasant hotels like *Alfonso a Mare (15 rooms | Via Marina di Praia | tel. 0 89 87 40 91 | www.alfonsoamare.it | Moderate)* with a good seafood restaurant. Disco goers also head to the Marina di Praia for the extremely popular *Africana (www.africanafamousclub.com)*.

A Vespa is undoubtedly the best way to tackle the winding bends of the crowded Amalfitana

View from the Hotel Le Sirenuse on to the Santa Maria Assunta dome

POSITANO

(134 C5) (⤳ E6) **A picture-perfect town of cube houses quaintly stacked on two hills that slope steeply down to the sea: a picturesque medley of flatly domed roofs, white, pink and pastel-coloured façades and sun-dappled loggias and balconies woven with bougainvilleas and wild roses.**

Across from the way lies *Li Galli*, a rocky archipelago of small islands, apparently the mythological home of the sirens from the Odyssey. The islands were once owned by ballet dancer Rudolf Nurejew, who spent his last summer here. Positano (pop. 4000) was a fishing village until the 1950s when it was discovered by the glamourous and the famous, in search of *la dolce vita*. The town boomed and even created its own fashion – *moda positano* – a style characterised by light, flowing fabrics in Mediterranean colours. Positano is also famous for its art scene and numerous galleries *(www.liquidart system.com)*.

SIGHTSEEING

SANTA MARIA ASSUNTA
This beautiful church, with its majolica dome, is on the main piazza. On the inside is a medieval painting of the Madonna while the outside has a relief portraying some fish, a fox and a sea monster, Positano's landmark. *Piazza Flavio Gioia*

FOOD & DRINK

DA ADOLFO
Fresh fish served at the water's edge in a picturesque bay. Boat shuttle service from the beach at Positano. With access to the beach club. *Daily in summer | Via Laurito*

40 | tel. 0 89 87 50 22 | www.
daadolfo.com | *Moderate*

DA VINCENZO
Vincenzo's speciality is *panzerottini mar-garet* dough pockets filled with ricotta, fresh basil and the small, sweet tomatoes from Furore. *Daily in summer | Via Pasitea 172–178 | tel. 0 89 87 51 28 | Budget–Moderate*

VALLE DEI MULINI
This family run restaurant is in a green secluded corner next to the stream which runs through the town. Delicious food and pizzas. *Daily in summer | Via Vecchia 5 | tel. 0 89 87 52 32 | www.ristorantevalledeimulini.it | Moderate–Expensive*

SHOPPING
Positano's centre is a pedestrian zone and its meandering *Via Pasitea* is lined with one boutique after another, all full of colourful summer fashions, sandals and bags. Everything is very casual, very elegant and far from cheap. Another option is to buy some of the local specialities: Campania wines, citrus marmelades and *limoncello,* the bright yellow lemon liqueur. The lemon and maquis fragrances of the Amalfitana are available in perfume form from *Profumi di Positano (Via Cristoforo Colombo 175 | www.profumidipositano.it).*

ENTERTAINMENT
Music on the rocks (www.musicontherocks. it) in a literal sense: disco and piano bar at the *Marina Grande* beach.

WHERE TO STAY
CASA GUADAGNO ⚜
Pleasant, reasonably priced guesthouse. *7 rooms | Via Fornillo 36 | tel. 0 89 87*

50 42 | www.pensionecasaguadagno.it | Budget

HOTEL REGINELLA ⚜
Ten very stylish rooms, most with sea views, in the centre of town. *Via Pasitea 154 | tel. 0 89 87 53 24 | www.reginellahotel.it | Moderate–Expensive*

SAN PIETRO ⚜
Fantastic luxury hotel built into the cliffs with splendid views, own elevator down to a private beach, cocktail terrace and starred restaurant. *58 rooms | Via Laurito 2 | tel. 0 89 87 54 55 | www.ilsanpietro.it | Expensive*

LOW BUDGET

Look out for the posters for the sagre, the summer food festivals – e.g. in July the *tuna festival* in Atrani or in the first week of August the *anchovy festival* in Cetara: here you can enjoy the local specialities at inexpensive prices.

For only 8 euros you can take an 80 minute trip with *Cooperativa Sant'Andrea's ferry (www.coop santandrea.com)* from Sorrento or Salerno to Amalfi; or the attractive Positano–Salerno route. The lovely ⚜ coastline view from the open deck comes free of charge.

The ● *Giardino della Minerva (Tue–Sun 9am–1pm | www.giardinodella minerva.it)* in Salerno was where the students from Italy's first medical faculty learnt how to heal with herbs and essences in the 14th century. The entrance fee is only 3 euros and it is a peaceful oasis in the midst of the hustle and bustle of the old town.

LE SIRENUSE ᨆ

Old summer palace converted into a boutique hotel, in the heart of Positano, with superb spa facilities. *60 rooms | Via Cristoforo Colombo 30 | tel. 0 89 87 50 66 | www.sirenuse.it | Expensive*

INFORMATION

Via Regina Giovanna 13 | tel. 0 89 87 50 67 | www.aziendaturismopositano.it

WHERE TO GO

MONTEPERTUSO/NOCELLE/SANTA MARIA DEL CASTELLO (134 C5) *(⊞ E6)*

From Positano you can also go on some mountain excursions such as walking up some rather steep stairs to ᨆ *Montepertuso,* 365 m/1197 ft above sea level (40 minutes), a little village with some very good *trattorias with spectacular views,* e.g. ᨆ *La Tagliata (April–Oct daily | Via Monsignor Vito Talamo | tel. 0 89 87 58 72 | www.latagliata.com | Budget–Moderate)* with three rooms or *Il Ritrovo | Nov–Jan closed Wed | Via Montepertuso 77 | tel. 0 89 87 54 53 | Budget–Moderate).* The very inviting *B&B Casa Cuccaro (6 rooms | Via Nocelle 2 | tel. 0 89 87 54 58 | www.casacuccaro.it | Budget)* has a lovely roof terrace and is in the traffic-free village of Nocelle. A stairway leads down to the Spiaggia d'Arienzo and the nice lido and good restaurant ● *Bagni d'Arienzo (www.bagnidarienzo.com).* From here you can take a private boat shuttle to Positano. Public buses commute between Positano and Nocelle. A typical tour takes you from Nocelle up the steep climb to the ᨆ *belvedere* at the small *Santa Maria del Castello* pilgrimage church. One of the Costa Divina's most beautiful hikes is the ᨆ *Sentiero degli Dei* mountain trail from Montepertuso via Nocelle to Agerola – also as circular route (see p. 71).

RAVELLO

(135 D5) *(⊞ F6)* **For many connoisseurs of the Costa Divina,** ᨆ **Ravello (350 m/1148 ft above sea level) is their favourite place. At Atrani the road branches off into the lush** *Valle del Dragone* **(valley of the dragon).**

The road winds up through forests and past terraces with olives, lemon groves and vines, especially vines as this coast is were some of the best grapes are grown. On the other side of the valley is Scala with its large Romanesque cathedral. During the Middle Ages Ravello had good connections with the Normans and the town prospered and today there is nothing provincial about its twelve churches, convents and villas – despite only having 2500 inhabitants. A few world-famous luxury hotels in impressive *palazzi* and enchanting ᨆ gardens with breathtaking views complete the picture.

SIGHTSEEING

DUOMO SAN PANTALEONE ★

A comprehensive restoration in 1975 restored the building to its original 11/12th century Romanesque architecture and removed all traces of the baroque. The influence of the Byzantine Norman culture is evident in the bronze door from the 12th century, in the mosaics of the *ambo* (lectern), as well as in the mosaics and reliefs on the pulpit (13th century). The left side altar houses the relics of the town's patron saint Pantaleone. The small *cathedral museum (daily 9am–7pm)* houses precious reliquaries and the 1272 marble bust of Sigilgaita Rufolo, a member of Ravello's Rufolo dynasty. *Piazza Duomo*

VILLA CIMBRONE

The villa of an English lord from 1904 is well located on the extreme edge of the cliff saddle on which Ravello lies. The highlight of the villa's large park – with avenues, hedges, flower beds, sculptures and little temples – is the lookout terrace ★ ● ᴬ̤ *Terrazza dell'Infinito* with a panoramic view of the coast. Today the villa houses an exclusive hotel and a Michelin-starred restaurant. *Park daily 9am–30 min before sunset | www.villacim brone.com*

VILLA RUFOLO

A solid entrance tower leads into this medieval villa that is done in an Arab-Sicilian style (pointed arches in the small courtyard) with its wonderful ᴬ̤ terrace garden above the coast with palms, pine trees and lovely views. In the 13th century this was the home of the wealthy Rufolo family, the villa became famous after Richard Wagner used it as the inspiration for the magical Klingsor garden in his opera "Parsifal". Prestigious concerts are held inside or on the terrace, where not only Wagner is played. The highlight is the Ravello Festival *(June–Sept | www.ravel lofestival.com)*. *Daily 8am–1 hr before sunset*

FOOD & DRINK

CUMPÀ COSIMO

A must for its highly acclaimed, delicious pasta dishes. It has the cosy ambience of a *trattoria* – but the prices are in a higher category. *Daily | Via Roma 44 | tel. 089 85 71 56 | Moderate*

SISINA'S SNACKBAR

Tasty *panini* and small appetizing snacks served with a view over to the neighbouring community of Scala. *Closed Sun | Piazza Fontana Moresca 2 | tel. 08985 82 03 | www.sisinas.it*

VILLA MARIA

Another dream location with lovely views is the comfortable ᴬ̤ terrace restaurant of the charming and traditional Villa Maria hotel. Tasteful, fresh traditional cuisine.

Surrounded by ivy and legends: the Villa Rufolo with terrace garden

Daily | Via Santa Chiara 2 | tel. 0 89 85 72 55 | www.villamaria.it | Moderate

WHERE TO STAY

HOTEL TORO
Friendly breakfast hotel at the cathedral with a beautiful garden. *10 rooms | Via Roma 16 | tel. 0 89 85 72 11 | www.hotel toro.it | Moderate*

VILLA SAN MICHELE
This small, charming hotel lies below Ravello right on the rocks overlooking the sea. *12 rooms | Via Carusiello 2 | tel. 0 89 87 22 37 | www.hotel-villasanmichele.it | Moderate*

INFORMATION

Via Roma 18 | tel. 0 89 85 70 96 | www. ravellotime.it

SALERNO

(135 E5) *(⌕ G5)* **The port and provincial capital (pop. 135,000) has experienced a revival over the years with its impressive fusion of medieval and contemporary 21st century architecture designed by renowned architects such as Zaha Hadid (Stazione Marittima) and David Chipperfield (Cittadella Giudiziaria).**
The town has hit the headlines for a variety of innovative ideas and projects ranging from its waste organisation scheme to cultural events such as its imaginative Christmas light installations. in the revived old town (starting point *Piazza Cavour)* with its wine bars, *trattorias* and beautiful shops. And it is full of students thanks to its acclaimed university, established in the Middle Ages from the prestigious Scuola Medica Salernitana.

SIGHTSEEING

CASTELLO ARECHI ☆
This imposing medieval fortification is built on top of a hill, with beautiful views over the city. A chic café serves refreshments, and various cultural events fill the castle with life. *Tue–Sun 9am–5pm | www.ilcastellodiarechi.it*

DUOMO DI SALERNO ★
When the city – under Robert il Giuscard, the ruler of the southern Italian Norman Kingdom – secured the relics of the Apostle Matthew in the 11th century, it had reason to build this impressive basilica with its valuable bronze portal, Byzantine mosaic and Romanesque masonry. *Mon–Sat 9.30am–6pm, Sun 4pm–6pm | Piazza Alfano Primo 1*

View over the Gulf of Naples to Mount Vesuvius from the Sorrento skyline

INSIDER TIP MUSEO DIOCESANO

The showpiece of the Diocesan Museum, behind the cathedral, is the largest medieval cycle of carved ivory panels. The 67 reliefs depict scenes from the Old and New Testament. *Daily 9am–1 hr before sunset | Largo Plebiscito 12*

FOOD & DRINK

HOSTARIA IL BRIGANTE

Simple *hosteria* with fresh, creative cuisine and good wines near the cathedral. *Closed Mon | Via Fratelli Linguiti 4 | tel. 32 83 42 34 28 | Budget*

INSIDER TIP OSTERIA CANALI

Slow Food restaurant near to the cultural and gastronomic centre in the old town. Special emphasis is placed on Cilento regional cuisine. *Closed Mon | Via Canali 34 | tel. cell 33 88 07 01 74 | www.osteriacanali.it | Moderate*

WHERE TO STAY

VILLA AVENIA

Six B&B rooms in a convivial old villa with an enchanting garden. *Via Tasso 83 | tel. 0 89 25 22 81 | www.villaavenia.com | Budget*

INFORMATION

Piazza Vittorio Veneto 1 (at the train station) | tel. 0 89 23 14 32 | www.eptsalerno.it

SORRENTO

(134 B5) (*Ø E6*) Sorrento (pop. 17,000) and its peninsula were, thanks to their fantastic location on a plateau high above the Gulf of Naples, "discovered" by the English in the 18th century and became a popular destination.

In the years to follow grand hotels, beautiful villas and lush parks were created. Some of these still stand and give Sorrento an old-world magic. Many new hotels have been added over time (and even camp sites) and there is the usual urban sprawl and traffic chaos. Sorrento is also a centre for the art of intricately

CHURCHES

The Romanesque *Santi Filippo e Giacomo* cathedral on the *Corsa Italia* has a façade that was added in 1924 and old and new inlay work in the interior and on the portal. The Arabic style *San Francesco* cloister is the site of summer concerts. The *Sant'Antonio* church hous-

Sedile Dominova: in the 16th century the town council met here, today it is local pensioners

detailed wood inlay or intarsia. And given its proximity to Naples, there is even a nightlife scene with discos and wine bars.

SIGHTSEEING

BELVEDERE AT VILLA COMUNALE ● ⚜

This splendid lookout terrace has panoramic views, it is in Sorrento's small city park, a former monastery garden.

es votive images of seafarers and a beautiful nativity scene.

MUSEO ARCHEOLOGICO GEORGES VALLET

The museum in the Piano di Sorrento district is in a beautiful old villa set in the heart of a wonderful ⚜ park. It displays finds from the prehistoric necropolis and ancient statues found in Roman bathing villas. *Tue–Sun 9am–7pm | Villa Fondi | Via Ripa di Cassano*

INSIDER TIP ## MUSEO BOTTEGA DELLA TARSIA LIGNEA

The Renaissance Palace Pomarici Santo-masi is in itself worth a visit, but it also has a remarkable collection of inlay work collected by the inlay producer Alessandro Fiorentino, along with some of his own design pieces. Here your eyes will learn to detect counterfeit from genuine inlay works. There is also a shop. *Daily 10am–5.30pm, April–Oct until 6.30pm | Via San Nicola 28 | www.alessandrofiorentino collection.it*

MUSEO CORREALE DI TERRANOVA ☼

In a villa with a wonderful lemon grove (which is worth a visit in itself because of the beautiful views from the belvedere) there is an eclectic and highly valuable collection of porcelains, rococo portrait miniatures, majolica, vases and archaeo-logical finds from antiquity. *Tue–Sat 9.30am–6.30pm, Sun 9.30am–1.30pm | Via Correale 50*

SEDILE DOMINOVA

In the 16th century aristocratic city coun-cillors held their meetings under this loggia, painted with frescos, today pen-sioners from the workers' union sit and play cards. *Via San Cesareo 72*

FOOD & DRINK

BAGNI DELFINO

Here you can enjoy delicious seafood dishes at a moderate price on the beach clifftops. *April–Oct daily | Via Marina Grande 216 | tel. 08 18 78 20 38 | Moderate*

IL BUCO

Excellent restaurant, in the converted wine cellar of an old monastery. That is what its name "the hole" alludes to. *Closed Wed | Seconda Rampa Marina Piccola 5 | tel. 08 18 78 23 54 | www.ilbucoristorante. it | Expensive*

GIGINO PIZZA A METRO

In the neighbouring town of Vico Equense this mega pizzeria (over 100 employees) is famous all over the Gulf. Historic place with varied menu. *Daily | Via Nicotera 15 | tel. 08 18 79 84 26 | www.pizzametro.it | Budget*

TORRE DEL SARACINO

Also in Vico Equense, famed Michelin starred chef Gennaro Esposito serves the very best Mediterranean cuisine. *Closed Sun evening and Mon | Via Torretta 9 | tel. 08 18 02 85 55 | www.torredelsaracino.it | Expensive*

SHOPPING

The maze of alleys in the old town (espe-cially *Via San Cesareo* and *Via Fusio*) are full of shops selling jewellery, gemstones, coral work, small antiques, embroidered table cloths and leather goods. A good time to shop in the traffic-calmed centre is in the evenings.

BEACHES

You can access the small, grey sandy beaches at the foot of the cliff plateau down steep stairs and serpentine pathways. The hotels, which line the cliff edge, have elevators down to the coast or you can take the public elevator at the Villa Com-munale. It is nicest at the fishing village *Marina Grande*. A beautiful coastline with access to the sea can be found towards *Punta del Capo* and at the *Marina di Puolo*.

ENTERTAINMENT

The central *Piazza Torquato Tasso* is the main meeting place; then stroll along the

Corso Italia and surrounding alleyways that are full of shops which are open late into the night in summer. If you are in the mood for a tarantella show, you will enjoy the *Fauno Notte Club* on the Piazza Tasso. An ambitious music club is *Artis Domus (Via San Nicola 56)* in an old villa. For aperitifs: *Photo Food & Drink (Via Correale 19)*.

WHERE TO STAY

CONCAPARK ◠◠ ◉
Comfortable hotel with view over Sorrento to the sea. One of Italy's first hotels to promote a "zero waste" policy. *200 rooms | Via Capo 8 | tel. 08 18 07 16 21 | www.concapark.com | Moderate–Expensive*

LA MINERVETTA ◠◠
Modern, Mediterranean-style hotel located in an amazing setting with panoramic views. *14 rooms | Via Capo 25 | tel. 08 18 77 44 55 | www.laminervetta.com | Moderate–Expensive*

SEVEN HOSTEL
A new generation hostel, without a whiff of youth hostel atmosphere, in Sant'Agnello. The Circumvesuviana train station is within easy walking distance. Comfortable double rooms, small dormitories and roof terrace with lounge atmosphere. Occasional live concerts in the bar. *Via Iommella Grande 99 | tel. 08 18 78 67 58 | www.sevenhostel.com | Budget–Moderate*

VILLA KETTY ◠◠
A delightful, well-furnished B&B with attentive and friendly owners in Vico Equense with swimming pool and sea view. The fruit served at breakfast is grown in the hotel's garden! *10 rooms | Via Comunale Scrajo 11 | tel. 32 97 34 28 20 | www.villaketty.com | Budget–Moderate*

VILLA TERRAZZA ◠◠
Art Nouveau villa with apartments, pool and breath-taking panorama located directly above Sorrento' harbour. *5 flats/suites | Via Luigi De Maio 38 | tel. 32 87 75 55 94 | www.villaterrazza.com | Moderate–Expensive*

INFORMATION

Via Luigi De Maio 35 | tel. 08 18 07 40 33 | www.sorrentotourism.com

WHERE TO GO

MONTE FAITO ◠◠ (134 C5) (*ଯ E5–6*)
In the summer months there is a *cable car (funivia)* to the summit (1131 m/370 ft) where there is a belvedere overlooking the Sorrento Peninsula, hikes and outdoor activities. The valley station is the Circumvesuviana station Castellamare di Stabia. The cable car is currently being overhauled and is scheduled to reopen in 2017. *www.eavsrl.it*

PUNTA CAMPANELLA/MARINA DEL CANTONE (134 B6) (*ଯ D–E6*)
After busy Sorrento the route continues (about 14 km/8.5 miles) at a more leisurely pace through the quiet countryside to the tip of the peninsula ◠◠ INSIDER TIP ▶ *Punta Campanella (www.puntacampanella.org)*, passing *Massa Lubrense (www.massalubrense.it)* with resort hotels and the small *Marina della Lobra* fishing port. Here you should visit Sorrento's INSIDER TIP ▶ oldest lemon grove, where they sell excellent *limoncello*, marmalades and the like at *Azienda Limoneto Il Gesù (Via IV Novembre 26b)*. From ◠◠ *Termini* you walk to the tip of the cape with wonderful views of Capri, the ravines and jagged cliffs, both the Salerno and Naples Gulf and the lighthouse *(there and back in about 3 hrs |*

www.giovis.it). Thanks to its rich marine life and natural fauna and flora the Punta Campanella is an *Area Naturale Marina*, a marine sanctuary.

The footpath that leads to the secluded, beautiful swimming bay *Baia di Ieranto* starts in *Nerano.* The next coastal village is the tranquil fishing village of **INSIDER TIP** *Marina del Cantone* with a long pebble beach, guesthouses and two famous restaurants: the first is *Taverna del Capitano (closed Mon/Tue | tel. 08 18 08 10 28 | www.tavernadelcapitano.it | Expensive)* right on the beach with 12 lovely rooms. The second is the elegant, gourmet restaurant, *Quattro Passi (closed Tue night and Wed | Via Vespucci 13 | tel. 08 18 08 12 71 | 7 rooms | www.ristorante quattropassi.com | Expensive).*

SANT'AGATA SUI DUE GOLFI ✂
(134 B5) (*E6*)

The gourmet tour continues above Sorrento, with even better views! The village (pop. 3000, 9 km/5.5 miles from Sorrento) is reached via a beautiful scenic road (SS 145) that has views of both the Gulf of Naples and the Gulf of Salerno and is home to possibly the best restaurant in southern Italy: the small, very fine ★ ● *Locanda Don Alfonso 1890 (closed Mon lunchtime and Tue lunchtime in summer, otherwise closed Mon/Tue | also 8 suites | Corso Sant'Agata 13 | tel. 08 18 78 00 26 | www.donalfonso.com | Expensive).* A few steps further and you'll find ❀ *Lo Stuzzichino (closed Wed | Via Deserto 1a | tel. 08 15 33 00 10 | www.ris torantelostuzzichino.it | Budget– Moderate),* where you can relax and enjoy a delicious Slow Food meal.

From Sant'Agata the route goes via Torca to the peaceful fishing bay ✂ *Marina di Crapolla.* Further along the SS 145 is *Colli di Fontanelle* and the simple, but good trattoria *Stelluccia (closed Wed | Via*

Nastro Azzurro 27 | tel. 08 18 08 35 25 | Budget) that also serves some tasty vegetarian dishes.

Above Sant'Agata is the agrotourism farm ❀ *Le Tore (8 rooms | Via Pontone 43 | tel. 08 18 08 06 37 | www.letore.com | Budget–Moderate),* which also supplies fruit and vegetables to the Michelin starred restaurant *Quattro Passi* in Marina del Cantone. Your wish is their command – very good! There are some lovely hikes that start right outside the front door.

Gourmets from Naples, Salerno and further afield all flock to Don Alfonso

PAESTUM & CILENTO

Paestum, with its Greek temples, lies in a broad plain roamed by the black buffalo that produce mozzarella, followed by a 50 km/30 miles wide forested hilly and mountain landscape that stretches down to the coast as far as the Gulf of Policastro. Sea, wind and rivers have formed a coastline that is dotted with rocky capes, grottos and stone arches. There are beaches with fine sand and crystal-clear water, where the dive conditions are as good as if you were on an island. Fishermen ferry the holiday-makers to numerous swimming coves. There are also sections of the Cilento coast that have long, sandy beaches that are ideal for families with children.

Santa Maria di Castellabate and Acciaroli both have an aura of elegance about them. In Marina di Camerota and in glamourous Palinuro, it is busiest in high season when all the Italians are on holiday. Holiday homes and hotels await the arrival of the guests and holiday resort bungalows and numerous camp sites are hidden in the shade of ancient olive trees. An alternative are the holiday homes on farms, because the charm of Cilento extends to the rural hinterland, with its farming villages, olive groves, vineyards, vegetable fields, its sheep and goat pastures, mountains, forests and river valleys. Here you can go hiking, cycling and enjoy the local *trattorias* all year round. The Parco Nazionale del Cilento *(www.cilentoediano. it)* – whose hinterland with the mountain range Monti Alburni and the Monte Cervati reaches summit heights of 1898 m/6227 ft – is now a Unesco World Heritage Site,

Ancient temples and enchanting coves: encounters with Greek gods, mysterious grottos and water buffalos

with its cultural treasures like the ancient sites of Paestum and Velia and the grand baroque Carthusian monestary, San Lorenzo, in Padula.

CASTELLABATE

(136 B6) (*ɷ J9) **Located at the northern tip of Cilento, the municipality (pop. 8200) consists of three districts:**
On a hilltop is the old Castellabate, in whose tranquil centre the holidaymakers

from the coast like to escape to on summer evenings. Or you stay up here in the nice guesthouse *Il Castello (12 rooms | Via Amendola | tel. 09 74 96 71 69 | www.ho telcastello.co.uk | Budget–Moderate)*. A good tip is also the *San Leo Cilentissimo* private estate *(6 apartments | Contrada San Leo | Budget)*. A neighbour sees to guests' needs and fresh rolls are delivered from the baker every morning. The two other communities are the coastal fishing villages of *Santa Maria di Castellabate* and *San Marco* that both lie on the sandy

Santa Maria, the seaside part of Castellabate, with its fishing harbour

beaches of Castellabate bay with the beautiful ☆ *Punta Licosa* headland in the south.

In the centre of Santa Maria, at the sandy beach harbour, people meet up in the evening to stroll under the imposing *palazzo* of the noble Perrotti family. You can also stay right on the beach, either in the lovely, small *Villa Sirio (34 rooms | Lungomare De Simone 15 | tel. 09 74 96 10 99 | www.villasirio.it |* Expensive*)* with elegant restaurant – popular for romantic weddings – or in the simpler *Grand Hotel Santa Maria (59 rooms | Via Senatore Manente Comunale 1 | tel. 09 74 96 10 01 | www.grandhotelsantamaria.it |* Moderate–Expensive*)* which has the perfect location overlooking the sandy beach. You can dine on fish dishes at *I Due Fratelli (daily in summer, otherwise closed Wed | Via Sant'Andrea | tel. 09 74 96 80 04 | Budget–Moderate)* 1 km/0.6 mile before Castellabate.

Right on the beach, nestled in fragrant greenery lies the *Trezene* holiday resort

(tel. 09 74 96 50 27 | www.trezene.com | Budget*)* with 40 bungalows, chalets and its own beach with games, sports and excursion offers. The family-run *Hotel Ristorante Da Carmine (26 rooms | Lungomare Alcide De Gasperi 37 | tel. 09 74 96 30 23 | www.albergodacarmine. it |* Budget–Moderate*)* right on the beautiful sandy bay of *Ogliastro* in the south of Castellabate is highly recommended. The Cilento is famous for its *fichi bianchi* – dried figs, filled with candied lemon peel and almonds – and the best are available in *Santa Maria* at the *Enoteca Casaburi (Corsa Matarazzo 52)*. The owner, Antonio Casaburi, also has some good Cilento travel tips for his clients.

WHERE TO GO

COASTAL RESORTS

Each place on the coast has its own character: bustling *Agropoli* **(136 B5)** *(ꔄ J8)* has a splendid position on the coast and its main road, Corso Garibaldi, is full of shops and cafés. In the ⚜ old town you can also climb up the long flight of steps to the castle with its fantastic views all the way to Capri. One of Agropoli's beaches is the popular *Baia di Trentova* 2 km/1.2 mile to the south. On the peninsula between Baia di Trentova and Santa Maria di Castellabate you can go for wonderful hikes. Feeling a little hungry? You can eat very well in Agropoli: the cheese selection is wonderful, especially the creamy buffalo mozzarella at the *La Veranda (closed Mon, July/Aug also for lunch | Via Piave 38 | tel. 09 74 82 22 72 | Budget–Moderate)* or the delicious stuffed calamari in the comfortably elegant gourmet restaurant *Il Ceppo (closed Tue | Via Madonna del Carmine 31 | tel. 09 74 84 30 36 | www.hotel ristoranteilceppo.com | Moderate)* on the periphery of the village with a small, nice hotel *(20 rooms | Budget)* across the road. Why not try one of the top local wines, e.g. from *Barone, Maffini,* or the wonderfully located *Azienda San Giovanni* or from *De Conciliis.* Popular for summer-hot disco nights with a magnificent view over the

sea is ⚜ *New Carrubo (www.newcarrubo. it)* in front of the old town.

After the Punta Licosa headland is **INSIDER TIP** *Acciaroli (138 A4) (Ⓜ J10)* with its stately stone houses right on the sea and harbour with a large fishing fleet, where wealthy Neapolitans moor their yachts in the summer. On the beach is the exceptionally beautiful hotel *Stella Marina (12 rooms | Via Nicotera 137 | tel. 09 74 90 47 25 | www.stellamarinahotel. com | Moderate).*

From Acciaroli it is on to ⚜ *Pollica* with fantastic views of the Cilento coast. A culinary tip – in the hills about 12 km/7.4 miles inland – in *San Mauro Cilento* is *Al Frantoio (daily in summer, otherwise only Fri evenings and Sat/Sun | Ortale | tel. 09 74 90 32 39 | Budget)* of the *Cooperativa Nuova Cilento (www.cilen toverde.com)* who produce one of the best 🌿 organic olive oils in Campania. The attached restaurant serves authentic regional cuisine.

Further along the coast is the village of *Pioppi* with pebble beach and cliffs. The

---

⭐ **Punta Licosa**
This headland in Castellabate is steeped in the legend of the sirens and ideal for long coastal hikes
→ p. 88

⭐ **Steep coast of Marina di Camerota**
The beautiful bays, coves and grottos along this rocky coast are ideal for swimming, best to combine a hike with a boat trip → p. 89

⭐ **Paestum**
Well-preserved Greek temples, the most vibrant frescos of antiquity – and afterwards fresh buffalo mozzarella → p. 91

⭐ **Grotte di Castelcivita**
Not a bad option when the weather is iffy: a visit to the most spectacular cave in the karst mountains of Cilento → p. 93

⭐ **Excursion boats**
The stuff of dreams: take a relaxing boat trip to some fantastic sea grottos and then enjoy a barbeque on the beach → p. 94

⭐ **Certosa di San Lorenzo**
The Carthusian monastery of Padula has the largest cloister in the world and is now a Unesco World Heritage Site → p. 96

MARCO POLO HIGHLIGHTS

17th century *Palazzo Vinciprova (Wed–Mon 9.30am–12.30pm and 4pm–7pm | Via Caracciolo 142)* has an interesting maritime museum and an exhibition about Mediterranean cuisine. *La Vela* family hotel *(50 rooms | Via Caracciolo 130 | tel. 09 74 90 50 25 | www.lavelapioppi.com | Budget–Moderate)* has a great location right on the beach and its own summery restaurant. A good place for some authentic Cilento cooking is INSIDER TIP *La Caupona (daily in summer, otherwise only Sat evenings | Via Caracciolo 2 | tel. 09 74 90 52 51 | Budget–Moderate)*. The owner was a personal friend of the American nutritionist Ancel Keys, who lived in Pioppi when he researched his work on the "Mediterranean diet". The pebbly beaches of Acciaroli and Pioppi are amongst the cleanest in the region and have frequently been awarded Blue Flag status.

If you enjoy sitting on the harbour, in order to eat freshly caught fish, then try the restaurant *Trattoria del Mar (in winter closed Mon | Via Angelo Lista 42 | tel. 09 74 90 77 44 | www.hotelilporto.com | Budget–Moderate)* in the hotel *Il Porto (13 rooms | Budget–Moderate)* in the neighbouring town *Marina di Casal Velino (138 A–B4) (￼ K10)*. In the hills above Casalvelinos is the ￼ INSIDER TIP *I Moresani (tel. 09 74 90 20 86 | www.agriturismoimoresani.com | Budget–Moderate)* holiday farm with riding stables, ten attractive guest rooms and a highly praised Slow Food kitchen. The ingredients are grown on the farm and guests can participate in cooking courses. If you don't like riding, you can use one of their bicycles.

PUNTA LICOSA ★ ☆
(136 A6) (￼ H9)

This rugged, maquis-covered headland with the little island, Isola Licosa, off its coast owes its name to Leucosia, one of the three sirens, who waited here for Odysseus. It is a wonderful landscape, with the shoreline and forested hills with and olive groves: a bucolic yet naturally wild landscape ideal for hikes. Divers and snorkelers however, will enjoy the rocky coast with its clear waters.

In *Ogliastro Marina* there are a few small hotels – simple, but stylish – right on the sea and with decent rooms that also serve delicious local cuisine, such as *Il Cefalo (8 rooms | tel. 09 74 96 30 19 | www.ilcefalo.it | Budget)* and *Da Carmine (30 rooms | Via Provinciale | tel. 09 74 96 30 23 | www.albergodacarmine.it | Budget–Moderate)*. From Ogliastro a pine grove leads down to the headland ☆ beach. If the access from Ogliastro is closed, you can take another walk (just as nice) to the cape and its lighthouse from the harbour of San Marco di Castellabate.

LOW BUDGET

You can enjoy an excellent *panini* in the *Alimentari Bufalina (Corso Matarazzo 155)* delicatessen in Santa Maria di Castellabate. It is cheaper than a meal in a restaurant. And often even more delicious.

It is not just all about tourism in the Cilento: in every village and in every town there are colourful weekly markets, where you can stock up cheaply with culinary or household goods.

MARINA DI CAMEROTA

(139 D6) *(M11–12)* **The road from Palinuro penetrates through rock promontories flanked by lovely beaches with fine sand on the one side and forested mountains rising up on the other.**

Marina di Camerota (pop. 3500) and Palinuro together are the main holiday area of southern Cilento and more and more camp sites and holiday resorts are springing up in the shadow of their olive trees and pines groves. It is an area of natural beauty and includes the ★ ⬝⚲ *steep coast of Marina di Camerota* between the Punta degli Infreschi in the south and Capo Palinuro with its bays, coves and countless grottos. A grotto at the *Mingardo* beach is the unusual venue for the atmospheric summer disco *Il Ciclope*.

FOOD & DRINK

LA CANTINA DEL MARCHESE
Sit between barrels of superb wine and enjoy the salami, ham and cheese from the local mountains. At weekends they serve the kinds of traditional local dishes that are seldom seen on menus: an institution. *Evenings in summer, Sat/Sun also lunchtime, otherwise only Fri/Sat evenings and Sun lunchtime | Via del Marchese 13 | tel. 09 74 93 25 70 | Budget*

INSIDER TIP IL PIRATA DI PORTO INFRESCHI
In the enchanting Baia degli Infreschi *(on foot about 2–2.5 hrs, or an excursion boat 10 euros)* you sit at wooden tables in the shade – the kitchen is in a grotto – and enjoy grilled *gamberoni*, fish soup, spaghetti with fresh anchovies, all delicious. If you pre-book, you can dine on a

Only accessible by boat – or after a long hike – Baia degli Infreschi

generous fish menu (*Expensive*) in the evening, including the boat transfer. *Only June–mid Sept lunch | tel. 33 35 91 74 13 | Budget*

ACTIVITIES, SPORTS & BEACHES

On old mule paths hikes lead into the mountains and forests in the hinterland,

MARINA DI CAMEROTA

through the rich flora of Cilento, where there is a unique type of primrose – the *primula palinuri* which only blooms in March/April – it is also the symbol of the national park. Or you can hike along the ⚲⚲ rocky coast with its wonderful views. It is a good idea to have the knowledgeable national park guide, Giacomo Ciociano, accompany you: *Assitur (Via Bolivar 17 | tel. 09 74 93 27 98 | www.assitur.com)*. The hike from *Marina di Camerota* to the beautiful *Porto degli Infreschi* bay (about 2–2.5 hours easy walking) is well-marked and is easy to find. The designated starting point is on the western end of the magnificent *Lentiscelle* beach, on the same level as the grotto. It is ideal to combine the tour with a boat ride. Excursion boats take you to the sea grottos that dazzle and glimmer with wonderful colours. In the summer the boats (about 10 euros) run regularly to the bays – accessible only from the sea or via long footpaths – from the harbour. Trips with fish barbeque on the beach during the day or in the evening – wonderfully atmospheric – are organised by the fishing cooperative, *Cooperativa Cilento Mare (tel. 33 98 87 79 90 | www.coopcilentomare.com)* at the harbour.

The hamlet of *Marina di Camerota* has a row of stunning beaches. To the west a dune beach stretches out for miles towards *Capo Palinuro*, immediately west of the village is the beautiful *Calanca* bay and east of the harbour the sandy *Spiaggia Lentiscelle* stretches out.

Favourite amongst divers are the underwater grottos *(www.divingcamerota.it)*. One of the tourism agencies, who facilitate the guided hikes, excursions, boat trips, accommodation, car rentals etc. is *Agenzia Infante Viaggi e Turismo (Lungamare Trieste 85 | tel. 09 74 93 29 38 | www.agenziainfanteviaggi.it)*.

WHERE TO STAY

CALANCA
Centrally located, friendly, family resort with good food that is right on the beautiful sandy beach of Calanca. Also eleven holiday apartments. *20 rooms | Via Luigi Mazzeo 60 | tel. 09 74 93 21 28 | www.hotelcalanca.com | Budget–Moderate*

HAPPY VILLAGE
The largest, most well-equipped (sailing, diving and surfing lessons, wellness area) and possibly the nicest holiday resort (bungalows) in an old olive grove on a lovely bathing bay. *257 apartments | Cala d'Arconte | tel. 09 74 93 23 26 | www.happyvillage.it | Moderate–Expensive*

INFORMATION
At the harbour | tel. 09 74 93 29 40 | www.prolococamerota.it

WHERE TO GO

CAMEROTA ⚲⚲
(139 D6) (∅ M11)
This old inland settlement 10 km/6 miles inland is situated picturesquely on a hilltop. In the summer a *craft market* takes place here every Wednesday evening *(6pm–midnight)* with typical products from the region such as earthenware jugs, ceramics, baskets and carvings made from of the wood of olive and carob trees. A legendary pizzeria is named after the typical pizza made of wholemeal flour and oregano: *Rianata a' Vasulata (closed lunchtime | Via San Vito 30 | tel. 09 74 93 54 27 | Budget)*.
In the village of *Licusati*, above Camerota, an imposing Renaissance *palazzo* offers charming, old-fashioned accommodation. The nearby farmstead (within walking distance) also belongs to them and you can

enjoy some delicious local cuisine there: *Palazzo Crocco (5 rooms | Largo Crocco | tel. 09 74 93 70 14 | www.palazzocrocco.it | Budget).*

SAPRI (139 F5) (*ⓘ N11*)

Pleasant coastal town (36 km/22 miles away, pop. 7000) with good beaches, charming coastal areas. On the 🏊 way to Sapri, a scenic drive with magnificent views of the mountains of Basilicata and Calabria, lies the pretty coastal village of INSIDERTIP *Scario* with its beautiful village church on the Piazza and an inviting seaside promenade. Scario does not have any beaches in the vicin-

The rugged, dramatic nature of the Cilento coastline at the Costa della Masseta

clear water, as well as restaurants serving traditional Campanian cuisine on the central Piazza Plebiscito: *'A Cantina i Mustazzo (daily | tel. 09 73 60 40 10 | www.cantinamustazzo.com | Budget)* and *Cantina r'u Ranco (closed Mon | tel. 09 73 60 37 06 | www.locandaariadelre. it | Expensive).* Sapri is on the Gulf of Policastro on the border of the Basilicata, which begins here with the Maratea coast, one of southern Italy's especially ity but that is no problem as excursion boats commute to the nicest bays, which dot the wild, rocky *Costa della Masseta* coast.

PAESTUM

(136 B4) (*ⓘ J8*) ★ At night illuminated by spotlights, the perfect temples look like the backdrop for a Hollywood movie,

while in daylight the Cilento mountains provide a majestic setting.

Uncovered under rampant vegetation in the 18th century, the site turned out to be the centre of a large city founded by the Greeks (6th century BC) and colonised by the Romans (3rd century BC): three massive, amazingly well-preserved temples, the remains of an amphitheatre, an agora (the

death is today used as Paestum's logo. *Daily 8.30am–7.30pm, closed 1st and 3rd Mon of the month | Via Magna Grecia 167 | www.museopaestum.beniculturali. it*

TEMPLES

Of the three Doric temples – which you have to imagine as being brightly painted

The best preserved of the three temples: Neptune's Temple (Tempio di Nettuno)

Greek assembly square) and the forum (Roman assembly square) as well as thick fortification walls from the 5th century BC.

SIGHTSEEING

MUSEO ARCHEOLOGICO NAZIONALE

The interesting museum displays items that once adorned the temple city: stone reliefs, terracotta statues, painted tomb stones and a sensational find: the *tomba del tuffatore,* a tomb with stone slabs with fresco paintings depicting a man diving into water from a tower The image of the symbolic jump from life to

and decorated with stone ornaments – the most beautiful and best preserved is the middle one (480–470 BC). Researchers now doubt the 18th century belief that this temple was dedicated to the Roman God Neptune. The oldest temple (530 B.C.), known as the Basilica, stands right next door and was supposedly dedicated to Hera. The last, the northern temple, was probably dedicated to Athena and is also called Ceres Temple. The foundations of a few Roman villas have been exposed in the residential area in the west of the facility. *Daily 8.45am–1 hr before sunset www.paestumsites.it*

FOOD & DRINK

NONNA SCEPPA

Filled artichokes, hearty pork, interesting fish dishes, chickpeas and shellfish: best traditional cuisine is served in this large, lively restaurant with a beautiful terrace near the temples. *Closed Thu and in winter except Sat evenings | Contrada Laura 45 | tel. 08 28 85 10 64 | www.nonnasceppa.com | Moderate*

RISTORANTE MUSEO

Going strong for decades – down-to-earth, decent meals at fair prices. Right next to the archaeological museum. *Closed evenings, Nov–March also Mon | Via Magna Graecia 921 | tel. 08 28 811135 | www.risto rantemuseo.it | Budget*

INSIDERTIP TENUTA SELIANO

Tasteful country estate with excellent local cuisine to order, also a good option for longer stays (14 rooms and swimming pool). Situated not far from the temples, near Capaccio. *April–Oct daily | tel. 08 28 72 36 34 | www.agriturismoseliano. it | Budget–Moderate*

SHOPPING

The plain of Paestum is the heartland of the rich, creamy *Mozzarella di Bufala* cheese and it is also where you can see the black, water buffalo in enclosures with ponds. There are sales points everywhere along the state road 18 towards Battipaglia, a good option is the ⊕ organic cheese factory *Caseificio Vannulo (Via Galileo Galilei 10 | Capaccio Scalo | www.vannulo.it).* You can also buy (and taste) organic mozzarella in all varieties at the INSIDERTIP *Fattoria del Casaro* estate *(Via Licinella 5 | tel. 08 28 72 27 04 | www. lafattoriadelcasaro.it | Budget)* with lovely garden near the temples. In addition to tasty souvenirs the *Bazar Cerere (Via Magna Graecia 849 | www.bazarcerere. com)* also sells old engravings.

WHERE TO STAY

MASSERIA LA MORELLA

Most of the hotels in and around Paestum are either massive complexes or small, tastelessly decorated B&Bs. This stylishly renovated estate from the 18th century stands in contrast and offers an idyllic setting near Battipaglia. Although the temples are 25 km/15.5 miles away, it is the perfect base from which to explore Campania. *6 rooms, 3 flats | SP 8 | tel. 08 28 51 00 08 | www.la-morella.it | Budget–Moderate*

SCHUHMANN

Pleasant hotel with its own beach, surrounded by a pine forest. *42 rooms | Via Marittima 5 | tel. 08 28 85 11 51 | www.ho telschuhmann.com | Moderate–Expensive*

WHERE TO GO

GOLE DEL CALORE (137 D5) (∅ L8)

The small gorge at the Fiume Calore near Felitto (which is about 50 km/31 miles inland) is a hiker's paradise with lots of spots where you can stop and enjoy a refreshing swim. The start and endpoint of the signposted circular route is the trattoria *Remolino (closed Mon | tel. 08 28 94 53 60 | Budget)* where you can enjoy your fill of homemade pasta and grilled chicken at very reasonable prices. In August Felitto honours the most famous pasta of the Cilento with a big festival: INSIDERTIP *Sagra del Fusillo (www.prolocofelitto.it).*

GROTTE DI CASTELCIVITA ★ ● (137 D3) (∅ L7)

This spectacular stalactite cave is n remarkable karst cave syster Alburni near Castelcivita (25 ` inland), in the Calore Val'

of 4 km/2.5 miles it is probably the largest and most diverse of the many caves in the Cilento. *Guided tours March–Oct daily 10.30am, noon, 1.30pm, 3pm, April–Sept also 4.30pm | www.grottedicastelcivita.com*

PALINURO

(138 C6) (*ω L11*) **Palinuro takes its name from the helmsman of Aeneas, legend has it that he died here in the surf and fierce winds off *Capo Palinuro* headland. Virgil wrote about it in the Aeneid.** The myth refers to real conditions: the winds around the cape must have always been difficult for sailors throughout the centuries. The area has a 2000-year history as evidenced by the ruins of the settlement of La Molpa on a hill on the southern part of the cape (also ruins of a medieval castle here). A short ☙ hike leads you there, and it is worth the effort for the breathtaking view. La Molpa may have been destroyed but Palinuro (pop. 1800) is now a lively summer holiday resort that has – along with Capo Palinuro – some wonderful beaches, such as *Baia del Buondormire, Spiaggia della Marinella* or *Cala del Cefalo.*

FOOD & DRINK

DA CARMELO
Palinuro's traditional restaurant in the Isca delle Donne district (with tasteful holiday apartments and rooms in the same house). *Daily | SS 562 | tel. 09 74 93 11 38 | www. ristorantebebdacarmelo.it | Moderate*

ᴇNDA AGRITURISTICA
᠈ᴇLLE DONNE
ᴜᴇ cooking with traditional Cilento
᠈ᴇ with home grown products:
᠈lami, cheese, honey, wine
᠈n attractive rural setting

in Isca delle Donne. *June–Sept daily, otherwise Sat/Sun | tel. 09 74 93 18 26 | www. iscadelledonne.com | Budget*

SHOPPING

The famous Cilento honey, the aromatic *miele di corbezzolo* (made from the blossoms of the strawberry tree shrub) is available in the nearby *San Mauro la Bruca:* INSIDER TIP ▸ *Azienda Agricola Prisco (Valle degli Elci | tel. 09 74 97 41 53 | www.agri turismoprisco.it | Budget–Moderate)* that also rents out six rooms and serves meals.

SPORTS & ACTIVITIES

EXCURSION BOATS ★
Boats for hire and excursion boats to the surrounding idyllic rocky bays and coves

᠈om

The impressive rock arch, Arco Naturale, on Capo Palinuro

(that are only accessible from the sea), to the spectacular grottos – blue, silver, blood-red – in the limestone coast of the Capo Palinuro and to the beautiful beaches or the evening beach barbeques are available through e.g. *Cooperativa Palinuro Porto (in the summer info kiosk at the harbour | www.palinurocoop.com).*

WHERE TO STAY

LA CONCHIGLIA ✪
Family-run four-star-hotel with good service, good cuisine made with fresh local products. Free bicycles for guests. The owners are committed to sustainable tourism and guests are welcome to help with the olive harvest. *30 rooms | Via Indipendenza 52 | tel. 09 74 93 10 18 | www. hotellaconchiglia.it | Moderate*

AZIENDA AGRITURISTICA SANT'AGATA ☘
Farm in a panoramic hill setting. Seven rooms, two cottages and campground; in the summer tasty cooking (only if pre-booked). *Via Sant'Agata Nord | tel. 09 74 93 17 16 | www.agriturismoantagata.net | Budget*

VILLAGGIO DEGLI OLIVI
White, Moorish-style bungalows amongst oleander, bougainvillea and olive trees; diving courses, sandy and rocky beaches. *Corso Pisacane 171 | tel. 09 74 93 85 01 | www.villaggiodegliolivi.it | Moderate*

INFORMATION

For the details of the co-ops who organise hikes and tours: *Piazza Virgilio 1 | tel. 09 74*

93 81 44. For accommodation information as well as organised tours to the places of interest in the hinterland: *Cilento Viaggi | Via Acqua dell'Olmo 248 | tel. 09 74 93 13 62 | www.cilentoviaggi.com*

WHERE TO GO

CERTOSA DI SAN LORENZO, TEGGIANO AND GROTTA DI PERTOSA

There is one bend after another as the road winds up into the mountains until it finally straightens out (after about 60 km/37 miles) and enters the *Vallo di Diano* where the wide plains of the river Tanagro are full of fertile fields. In the lovely little town of *Padula* (139 F2) (*m O8*) lies the ★ *Certosa di San Lorenzo (Wed–Mon 9am–7pm),* the largest Carthusian monastery in Italy, founded in 1300. In the 17th century it was vastly extended in an elegant baroque style: frescos and wooden and mother-of-pearl inlays decorate the chapels and church-es, and majolica tiles adorn the inviting kitchen. Today the monastery is a Unesco Site that attracts 350,000 visitors annually.

Within its walls is the *Museo Archeologico della Lucania Occidentale* with finds from the Cilento. In the summer theatre performances and concerts take place here, and from September INSIDER TIP▶ renowned exhibitions of contemporary art. There is also a tourist information office in the monastery *(www.comune. padula.sa.it).*

At the gates of the monastery you will find the unpretentious *Trattoria Do'Ngiulino (closed Fri | Viale Certosa | tel. 0 97 57 73 35 | Budget)* serving tender grilled lamb, excellent pizza and a wonderfully rich local wine. And in the evening there is the INSIDER TIP▶ lively palazzo, decorated with frescos and mosaics, in the centre of Padula: *Villa Cosilinum (24 rooms | Corso Garibaldi | tel. 09 75 77 86 15 | www.villacosilinum.it | Moderate)*

Panoramic terrace belonging to the charming Hotel Marulivo which was once a monastery.

with restaurant. Padula is famous for its excellent durum wheat bread and one of the best places to try it is the ⓦ Slow Food bakery *L'Antico Forno (SS 19, km 80.5 mark)* below the town.

Further north-west is the charming old town of ⚞ *Teggiano* (139 E2) *(ⓜ N8)* with a restored castle and numerous lovely churches. The active tourism cooperative, *Paradhosis (tel. 097 57 90 53 | www. paradhosis.it)*, offers tours and guides, their contact point is the *Museo Diocesano (Mon–Fri 9am–1pm | Piazza Valentino Vignone)*. The small natural history museum *Museo delle Erbe (Mon–Sat 9am–1pm and 3pm–7pm | Piazza della Santissima Pietà)* is on par with the Chiesa di San Francesco and guides one through the medieval herbal remedies and the expertise of the medical school of Salerno which was quite cutting-edge in its day.

You can enjoy a bowl of freshly prepared pasta at *Locanda dei Baroni (daily | Via San Francesco d'Assisi 68/70 | tel. 09 75 58 73 09 | www.locandadeibaroni. eu | Budget)*, the hotel next door, *La Congiura dei Baroni (10 rooms | Via Castello 4 | tel. 097 57 90 44 | www.lacon giuradeibaroni.it | Budget)*, has some inviting rooms. A further 20 km/12.5 miles north is Polla and the *Grotta di Pertosa* ((137 F3) *(ⓜ M7)*, March–Oct daily 9am–7pm, Nov–Feb 9am–4pm | www.grottedipertosa-auletta.it)*, another spectacularly magical stalactite cave, formed by an underground river, and accessed by excursion boat.

INSIDER TIP PISCIOTTA ⚞
(138 B5) *(ⓜ L10–11)*

This hamlet on a hilltop by the sea 10 km / 6.2 miles to the north would be even more picturesque if were not for the street concrete pillars – which tarnish the first impression – nevertheless, the streets and alleys of this medieval old

town are off limits to traffic and you can stay in four tasteful ⚞ holiday apartments with magnificent views: *Casa Pixos (Via Canto del Gelso 22 | tel. 09 74 97 37 92 | www.casapixos.it | Moderate)*. For a more luxurious option there is the charming ⚞ *Marulivo Hotel (11 rooms | Via Castello | tel. 09 74 97 37 92 | www.marulivohotel.it | Budget– Moderate)* in the restored apartments of a medieval monastery at the foot of the castle. Boat trips and cooking and ceramics courses are offered to their guests.

There are several excellent trattorias in the area such as the *Osteria del Borgo (April–Oct daily | Piazzetta dei Caduti | tel. 09 74 97 01 13 | Budget)* serving delicious food and traditional dishes from Cilento. Situated 2 km/1.2 mile from the centre (shuttle bus available) is the INSIDER TIP *Enoteca Per Bacco (June– Oct daily, April/May only Fri–Sun | Contrada Marina Campagna 5 | tel. 09 74 97 38 89 | www.perbacco.it | Budget–Moderate)* in a paradise setting surrounded by olive groves.

This town has a small train station and a fishing village down by the sea, which specialises in fishing anchovy *(alici)*. These (and other fish) are deliciously prepared at the ⓦ Slow Food *Ristorante Angiolinu (April–Oct daily | Via Passariello 2 | tel. 09 74 97 31 88 | Budget–Moderate)* by the sea.

VELIA **(138 B4)** *(ⓜ K10)*
Beyond Ascea are the impressive ruins of Velia, once a significant Greek port city. The sprawling archaeological site includes the remains of an acropolis, theatre, thermal baths, residential buildings and the *Porta Rosa* – the only perfectly preserved Greek archway from 4th century BC – and covers an area twice as large as that of Paestum. *Daily 9am–1 hr before sunset*

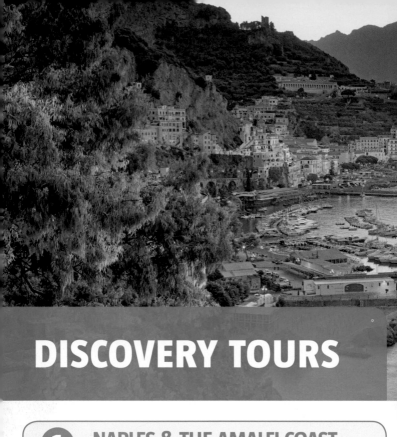

DISCOVERY TOURS

1 NAPLES & THE AMALFI COAST AT A GLANCE

START: **1** Naples END: **19** Scario	**9 days** Driving time (without stops) approx. 10–15 hours
Distance: ➡ a good 400 km/249 miles	

COSTS: approx. 1500–1600 euros for 2 people (hire car, petrol, accommodation, admission fees, train and ferry tickets; excluding the cost of food)

WHAT TO PACK: hiking boots, swimwear

IMPORTANT TIPS: The climb up Mount Vesuvius should only be attempted on relatively clear days.
There is usually heavy traffic along the "Amalfitana" at weekends. Always book accommodation in advance during the main holiday season.

Every corner of the earth has its own special charm. If you want to explore all the many different facets of this region, head off the beaten track or get tips for the best stops, breathtaking views, hand-picked restaurants or the best local activities, then these customised discovery tours are just the right thing. Choose the best route for the day and follow in the footsteps of the MARCO POLO authors – well-prepared to navigate your way to all the many highlights that await you along the tour.

From Naples in the north to the Cilento in the south, this tour takes you to remnants of 3500 years of Neapolitan history as well as mountains and beaches. Highlights include an excursion to the island of Procida, a climb up Mount Vesuvius and a trip along the legendary Amalfi Coast.

Once you have explored ❶ **Naples** → p. 32, take the **suburban Cumana line to Pozzuoli. On your way, stop off in Agnano** to visit the historic thermal baths ❷ **Terme di Agnano** → p. 43 **before continuing on the Cumana line to Pozzuoli. The short ferry trip to the charming island of**

DAY 1

❶ Naples

10 km/6.2 mi

❷ Terme di Agnano

19 km/11.8 mi

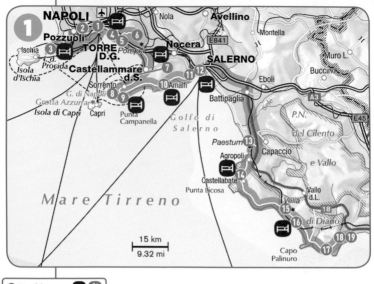

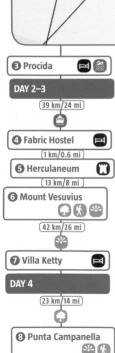

③ Procida 🛏 🏊

DAY 2–3

🚗 39 km/24 mi

🚢

④ Fabric Hostel 🛏

1 km/0.6 mi

⑤ Herculaneum 🏛

13 km/8 mi

⑥ Mount Vesuvius 🏛 🥾 ❄

42 km/26 mi

⑦ Villa Ketty 🛏

DAY 4

23 km/14 mi

⑧ Punta Campanella ❄ 🥾

7 km/4.3 mi

⑨ Marina del Cantone 🏊 🍴 🛏

③ Procida → p. 64 is a mini-cruise at a budget price. Stay the night on the island at **La Casa sul Mare** with views over the **Corricella beach**.

After spending the morning at the beach, **take the ferry back to Naples in the afternoon and then drive south to Portici** where you can spend the night at the **④ Fabric Hostel → p. 53**. In the morning visit the antique **⑤ Herculaneum → p. 50**, which is a lot less visited than Pompeii and far better preserved. Like Pompeii, Herculaneum was buried in volcanic pyroclastic flows from **⑥ Mount Vesuvius → p. 56. The scenic road from Torre del Greco goes up 1000 m/3280 ft;** put on your hiking boots and continue on foot to the edge of the crater where you will be treated to magnificent views over the Gulf of Naples! **From the motorway, the SS 145 takes you through coastal scenery to Sorrento. Take the exit at Vico Equense** and spend the night at the idyllic **⑦ Villa Ketty → p. 82**.

Drive through Sorrento and take the SP 7 past lemon and olive groves to Termini. Hikers will enjoy the **⑧ Punta Campanella → p. 82** with its excellent views of Capri. **A road ends at the ⑨ Marina del Cantone → p. 83 –** a picturesque seaside resort straight from the 1950s. The **Taverna del Capitano** offers guests a magical setting.

The **winding Amalfitana coastal road, the SS 163,** is an adventure in itself. Stop along the route to grab some fantastic photo opportunities! Positano, Praiano, Amalfi and Atrani – you are spoilt for choice among these picturesque towns. The best ice cream along the coast can be found in the **Gelateria Porto Salvo** *(Piazza Duomo)* in ⑩ **Amalfi → p.67**, where you can also spend the night at the **Residenza Luce**. **The Costa Divina ends in** ⑪ **Vietri sul Mare → p. 72** – here it is difficult to resist the temptation of buying some of the ceramics produced in the region. The neighbouring town of ⑫ **Salerno → p. 78** is witnessing a revival: medieval houses sit comfortably next to 21st century buildings. The town has also received acclaim for a variety of programs such as its waste scheme and cultural events. Spend the night in Salerno at the **Villa Avenia**.

Head off early next morning **to the Cilento.** Visit the spectacular Greek temples in ⑬ **Paestum → p. 91** and do not miss the opportunity to visit the interactive museum. A great place to take a break and enjoy some of the best buffalo mozzarella is at the **Rivabianca** cheese dairy *(www.rivabianca.it)* **on your right along the SS 18.** South of Agropoli the olive grove hills stretch all the way to the sea, interrupted by sandy coves such as at ⑭ **Santa Maria di Castellabate → p. 85**. Take a stroll around the centre of **Castellabate** on the top of the hill which has been awarded as the "most beautiful historic centre" on several occasions before staying the night at the seaside hotel **Villa Sirio**.

The drive along the coastal road takes you through Acciaroli, Pioppi and Marina di Ascea – one coastal town more beautiful than the next! Take a break for a dip in the sea on the golden sandy beach at ⑮ **Ascea** while also admiring the sea lily found here in high summer. The sea's water quality is regularly awarded the Blue Flag. After your time at the seaside, spend the night in **Pisciotta → p. 97** among the olive groves at Hotel ⑯ **Marulivo**.

But paradise goes on: at the wild and romantic ⑰ **Costa degli Infreschi**, which is best explored twice; once on foot and again by boat to hire **at the port in Marina di Camerota: Noleggio Barche Saturno** *(www.nolobarchesaturno.it)*. Afterwards the route **snakes up to Lentiscosa. Just before San Giovanni a Piro it is worth taking a detour to** ⑱ **Belvedere Ciolandrea**. Get your hiking boots on again here to explore one of the trails (unfortunately not well

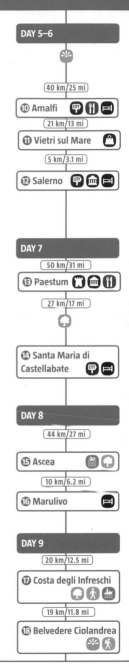

9 km/5.6 mi

⑲ Scario

signposted) before ending the tour in style at the chic seaside hamlet of ⑲ **Scario** → p. 91 with a well-earned aperitif at **Lungomare Marconi** in the historic **Bar Mosè**.

2

GOLDEN AGE AROUND CASERTA AND CAPUA

START: ❶ Caserta END: ❻ Caserta Vecchia	1 day Driving time (without stops) approx. 1–1 ½ hrs.
Distance: ➡ approx. 40 km/25 miles	

COSTS: around 30 euros per person for admission fees, plus petrol and food

IMPORTANT TIPS: The best day to take this tour is Thursday: The museum in ❸ **Capua** is only open in the afternoon on Tuesdays and Thursdays, the palace in ❶ **Caserta** is closed on Tuesdays. Make sure you book a table at ❻ **Caserta Vecchia**!

This tour takes you to one of the most historic areas in southern Italy: the second largest Roman amphitheatre in Italy and the gigantic Royal Bourbon Palace are reminders of the golden age of the Gulf of Naples. Spend a whole day immersing yourself in the region's history with its architectural highlights and discover Italy's south side with breathtakingly beautiful landscape.

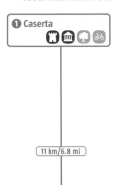

❶ Caserta

11 km/6.8 mi

08:30am Start your tour in the provincial capital city of ❶ **Caserta** (pop. 78,000) **approximately 20 minutes' drive away from Naples on the A1 northbound to Rome.** The gigantic royal palace of the Bourbons, the **Reggia di Caserta** *(Wed–Mon 8.30am–7.30pm),* is commonly known as the "Versailles of the south". Sprawling over 44,000 m²/10 acres, the palace was completed by the Italian-Flemish master builder Luigi Vanvitelli in 1773 after spending over 20 years working on this dream home for the Neapolitan king. Built to showcase grandeur and power, this late-Baroque palace draws half a million visitors each year and was used as a set for films including one from George Lucas' Star Wars trilogy. The INSIDER TIP **Terrae Motus** collection is particularly worth seeing with works from contemporary artists such as Joseph Beuys, Jannis Kounellis, Gilbert & George and many others, e.g. on the subject of the heavy earthquake which hit southern Italy in 1980.

Do not miss the expansive **park gardens** *(Wed–Mon 8.30am–2 hours before sunset)* located behind the palace! The long straight avenues and large fountains with tiered water cascades stand in direct contrast to the unbridled forests and Caserta's rugged northern mountains. The very romantic English Garden surprises visitors at the back of the park. The park's long stretches of tarmac avenues invite tourists to hire bikes at the entrance to the park and explore the gardens by bike (children's bikes and tandem bikes are also available).

01:00pm **After around 20 minutes along the SS 7 you'll reach ② Santa Maria Capua Vetere → p. 47,** one of the most important cities in Italy during the Roman era. In its well-maintained **amphitheatre** (the largest outside Rome) there was once a famous Roman gladiator school. Enjoy lunch in the excellent organic restaurant 🌿 **INSIDERTIP** ▶ **Amico Bio Spartacus Arena** *(daily | Piazza 1° Ottobre | tel. 0 82 31 83 10 93 | www.spartacusarena.it | Budget– Moderate)* **right next door to the amphitheatre.**

After a break for lunch, your journey takes you on to Capua through the flat, fertile plain of the Volturno River in front of the impressive volcanic arcs of the Campanian Apennines in the background. Thanks to the mild climate and the rich volcanic soil it has always been Campania's vegetable garden; the lush, dense vegetation still holds some fascination today, even though it has been spoilt in many areas by the

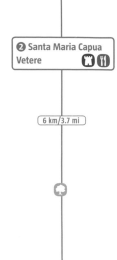

② Santa Maria Capua Vetere

6 km/3.7 mi

km/3.7 mi

Sant'Angelo
Formis

9 km/5.6 mi

⑤ San Leucio

10 km/6.2 mi

⑥ Caserta Vecchia

ugly urban sprawl. ❸ **Capua** → p. 47, a Roman settlement on the Via Appia and once the capital city of a Lombard principality, is today a small vibrant town with attractive baroque facades in the **town centre**. Do not miss the **Museo Campano** with its unusual collection of pre-Roman art and cult objects. The **district of ❹ Sant'Angelo in Formis** → p. 47 **in the north-east** is also worth a visit for its pre-Roman Benedictine abbey with splendidly preserved frescoes and its magnificent setting even for non-church goers.

04:00pm Now head along the SP 4 and the SS 87 to ❺ **San Leucio**, once the famous royal silk factory with the early industrial worker settlement **Quartiere San Carlo**. Today you can visit the restored royal grounds, the **Complesso Monumentale Belvedere San Leucio** (guided tours Wed–Mon 9.30am–5pm, Tue 9.30am–noon), with its museum exhibiting the silk manufacturing industry, a baroque garden and fantastic panoramic views over the plains of Caserta. Traditional silk scarves and products are also available in the museum's store **INSIDER TIP** **Piazza della Seta** (Mon–Sat 9.30am–8pm, Sun 9.30am–2pm | Via Antonio Planelli 1 | www.piazzadellaseta.com).

Return to the SS 87 and head in the direction of Caserta, taking the first left onto the Via dei Giardini Reali/Via Gennaro Papa where you'll reach the picturesque medieval hamlet of ❻ Caserta Vecchia, up in the hills offering amazing views over the plain, Mount Vesuvius and the haze or lights of Naples. With its inviting trattorias, cafés and artisan shops, Caserta Vecchia is a popular and vibrant destination especially at weekends. The perfect way to finish this tour is at 🌐 **Gli Scacchi** (Closed Mon | Via San Rocco 1 | tel. 08 23 37 10 86 | Moderate) recommended by the Slow Food guide. **Located to the east of the town,** the restaurant serves carefully prepared dishes made from local ingredients.

"Versailles of the south": late-baroque splendour in the Reggia di Caserta

THROUGH CILENTO'S KARST LANDSCAPE

START: ❶ Polla	3 days
END: ⓫ Teggiano	Driving time
Distance:	(without stops)
➡ approx. 250 km/155 miles	approx. 6–8 hrs.

COSTS: approx. 380 euros/2 people (accommodation, petrol, horse ride, admission fees)
WHAT TO TAKE: hiking boots, sun protection, water and a hiking map

IMPORTANT TIPS: book accommodation and the horse ride in advance at the ❺ VICA horse club!

Although famous for its beaches, the Cilento region also has a lot to offer inland. This tour takes you through karst limestone mountains, into limestone caves and through gentle river plains. The highlight is the impressive baroque Carthusian monastery of Padula.

Start your tour in ❶ Polla which is easily accessible over the A3 along a scenic mountain route to **❷ Sant'Angelo a Fasanella** where you can visit the impressive, early-medieval **San Michele** grotto church, with its caves full of altars as well as paintings and frescoes from the 14th/15th century. **Just 15 km/9 miles away to the northwest** of the church is the equally impressive **❸ Castelcivita stalagmite cave → p. 93** which is well worth the trip down underground. Spend the night in green surroundings at the delightful **❹ Antico Casolare** *(6 rooms | Contrada Suvcro 14 | tel. 08 28 77 29 85 | www.agriturismoanticocasolare.it | Budget)* where you can enjoy the excellent house wines and honey, jams and olive oil all produced by the family.

Set out the next morning on horseback along the Calore River: **Drive along the SS 488 to Castel San Lorenzo to the ❺ VICA horse club** *(Via Varco della Taverna | tel. 32 90 45 26 77 | www.trekkingacavallo.it).* This horseback ride includes a delightful picnic break next to the river. **Your route then carries on to ❻ Roscigno Vecchia**: Take a stroll through this desolate village which had to be evacuated at the beginning of the 20th century due to a landslide. This "19th century Pompeii" is today an interesting excursion in picturesque surroundings. One of the most interesting

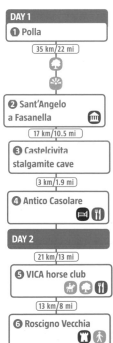

DAY 1
❶ Polla
35 km/22 mi
❷ Sant'Angelo a Fasanella
17 km/10.5 mi
❸ Castelcivita stalagmite cave
3 km/1.9 mi
❹ Antico Casolare

DAY 2
21 km/13 mi
❺ VICA horse club
13 km/8 mi
❻ Roscigno Vecchia
13 km/8 mi

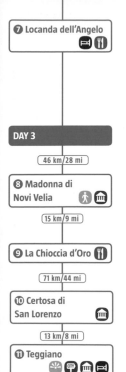

⑦ Locanda dell'Angelo

DAY 3

46 km/28 mi

⑧ Madonna di Novi Velia

15 km/9 mi

⑨ La Chioccia d'Oro

71 km/44 mi

⑩ Certosa di San Lorenzo

13 km/8 mi

⑪ Teggiano

culinary destinations is hidden away **in the Valle dell'Angelo:** The **⑦ Locanda dell'Angelo** *(3 rooms | Piazza Canonico Jannuzzi 2–3 | tel. 09 74 94 20 08 | www.confusi-mafelici.it | Budget)* **in the middle of the small village** offers simple accommodation and a very warm welcome. Its Slow Food affiliated ✪ **Osteria La Piazzetta** *(daily | Moderate)* serves refined Cilento cuisine using ingredients from the restaurant's own garden or from local farmers.

From Novi Velia the road takes you through dense forests up to a height of 1500m/4920ft where it is a short walk to the significant **⑧ Madonna di Novi Velia** sanctuary on the holy **Monte Sacro** mountain (also called Monte Gelbison). This 15th century church is one of the most important traditional worshipping sites for Cilento's miners and shepherds. **In Massa at the junction to Novi Velia is ⑨ La Chioccia d'Oro** *(Closed Fri | tel. 0 97 47 00 04 | Budget)* which serves tasty, very reasonably priced lunchtime meals.

The route now winds through Laurito, Rofrano and Sanza to Padula and the large baroque complex of **⑩ Certosa di San Lorenzo → p. 96**. In the 15th century the monks drained the swampy plains of the Vallo di Diano, now a fertile agricultural landscape. The charmingly small town of **⑪ Teggiano → p. 97** with castle, countless churches and stately medieval buildings offers breath-taking views of the surrounding region. Treat yourself at the end of this tour

Embedded into the karst of Cilento: the splendid San Michele grotto church

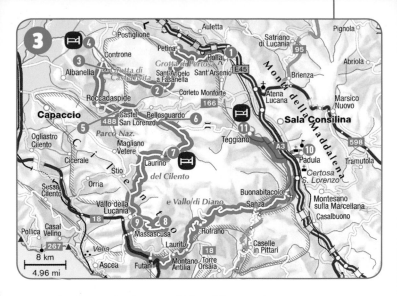

to a majestic stay at the elegant **Antichi Feudi** *(13 rooms |
Via San Francesco 2 | tel. 09 75 58 73 29 | www.antichifeudi.
com | Budget–Moderate)!* The owners have breathed new
life into this old baronial palace.

④ BIRD'S EYE VIEW FROM CAPRI'S HIGHEST PEAK

START: ❶ Marina Grande
END: ❼ Lo Smeraldo

1 day
Walking time
(without stops)
approx. 3 hours

Distance:
➡ 10 km/6.2 miles

Diffculty:
▂▃▅ medium

COSTS: a good 15 euros per person (cable car, bus, admission to the
Lo Smeraldo lido)
WHAT TO PACK: hiking boots, sun protection, drinking water,
swimwear, picnic, binoculars if you like

IMPORTANT TIPS: Do not attempt this route on rainy days. If you are
unsure about the weather, contact the tourist office *(tel. 08 18 37 06 86)*.
You must have a good sight, steady footing, a head for heights and be
in good condition to attempt this climb.

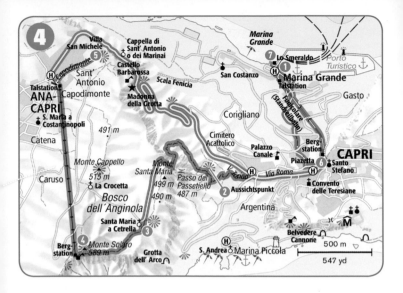

Explore the beauty of Capri from above: A hiking trail dating back centuries takes you to the highest peak on the island offering breathtaking panoramic views and explore the island's landmarks of Anacapri and Capri.

❶ Marina Grande 🚠

1700 m/5577 ft

❷ viewpoint ☀

09:00am From **❶ Marina Grande** take the cable car up to the town of Capri. Once you reach the end of the Via Roma, take the footpath on the left of the hospital entrance (Via Torina). This footpath and one another path used to be the only routes connecting Capri and Anacapri until late into the 19th century. **The path continues steadily uphill and once you leave the town, the path is occasionally signposted in red. After around ten minutes, you'll notice a junction to the right:** This leads you to a promontory with olive trees and the first spectacular **❷** INSIDER TIP **viewpoint.**

09:45am Continue through a holm oak forest. **Once you have reached the high clifftops,** you will be treated to the first panoramic views across the island and out to sea. It is less than half an hour from this point to a high plain near the hermitage ❸ **Santa Maria a Cetrella** standing at a height of 495 m/1624 ft. This paradise setting is the perfect spot for a picnic break and the island's highest peak, the 589 m/1932 ft high ❹ **Monte Solaro**, is now in close reach. **At the top of the mountain you will find the chairlift station from where you can enjoy a comfortable ride down to the centre of Anacapri. Go along the touristy Via Capodimonte** with its souvenir shops to ❺ **Villa San Michele**, which again offers amazing views of the region.

12:30pm **Returning to Anacapri's Piazza Vittoria, take the bus back to Capri. The bus terminates at the** ❻ **Piazzetta**, where you can spot the international jetsetters who meet up here in summer. **On the right-hand side of the Campanile between the two bars, stroll down the Via Acquaviva set of stairs to the Marina Grande.** Treat yourself to lunch at the ❼ **Lo Smeraldo** *(Easter–Sept daily | Piazza Vittoria | tel. 08 18 37 72 12 | www.losmeraldocapri.it | Moderate)* lido at the seaside where you can enjoy the afternoon (sun-)bathing and the evening sunset when the red sun literally falls into the sea.

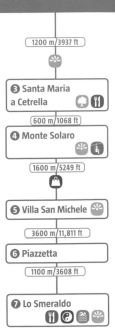

1200 m/3937 ft

❸ Santa Maria a Cetrella

600 m/1068 ft

❹ Monte Solaro

1600 m/5249 ft

❺ Villa San Michele

3600 m/11,811 ft

❻ Piazzetta

1100 m/3608 ft

❼ Lo Smeraldo

The view from the Villa San Michele stretches to the Sorrento peninsula

SPORTS & ACTIVITIES

Those keen for some exercise can work up a sweat just from a stroll through Positano: there are steep steps throughout the village.

Down here in the sultry heat of the south the approach to sports is more easy-going than it is up in the sports-mad north (especially in the upper Adriatic Sea near Rimini) but at the Gulf of Naples and in the Cilento there are plenty of options for the sporty and the energetic. Typical beach activities such as beach volleyball are possible on the wide sandy beaches of Paestum, Marina di Ascea, Marina di Camerota and Palinuro in the Cilento. They are also offered at the many campsites and holiday resorts that lie right on the beach.

Especially the Amalfi Coast, Capri, Ischia and the wildly romantic Cilento are ideal for excursions into nature – whether on foot, by bicycle or on horseback – outdoor and nature tour operators have for quite some time had this mountainous landscape on offer (e.g. *www.cilento-travel.com/en.html*, *www.italimar.com/en* and *www.genius-loci.it*). The tourist information bureaus provide contacts for bicycle rentals, riding stables and tour guides. For additional information about an active Cilento holiday visit *www.walking-trekking.com* which covers each section of the Cilento in great detail.

Photo: Sentiero degli Dei coastal walk above the Amalfi coast

Not just a diver's paradise: explore the wildly romantic Cilento on horseback, on mountain bike, by canoe or on foot

CYCLING

With its well-built network of roads and quieter traffic conditions, the Cilento region is a more relaxed alternative to Mallorca for keen cyclists. The bicycle shop *Ciclidea (SS 18 km 90 | tel. 08 28 72 35 64 | www.ciclidea.eu)* in Capaccio Scalo is an excellent place to visit where Pino Giovinal is on hand with some good tips.

HIKING

There are plenty of beautiful hiking areas to choose from in Campania. One of these is the island of Ischia with its Monte Epomeo; another area is the Monti Lattari *(www.parcoregionaledei montilattari.it)* mountain range with Monte Faito, which rises up inland from the Sorrento Peninsula. The Amalfi Coast has numerous paths (often old mule paths) that are ideal for hikes. They may be steep and rocky in parts but the reward is the magnificent views from the vantage points. And finally, there is the Cilento with its pristine, mountainous landscape – as yet undiscovered by tourists – with interesting ridge walks over the Monti Alburni mountains or on the Monte Cervati, or you can hike on Monte Sacro's devotional paths (it is also known as Monte Gelbison) to the Madonna sanctuaries. The tourist offices provide help with route maps and addresses of hiking organisations. Good websites with hiking routes, tips and contacts are *www.amalficoastrekking. com/en/list-of-hikes.html*, *www.car totrekking.com*, *www.capritrails.com*, *www.pithecusa.com*, *www.giovis.com* and *www.everytrail.com* (search under Campania).

HORSEBACK RIDING

In Cilento you can experience wonderful outrides on horseback, along the beaches, in the Mediterranean maquis, but especially in the lush forests of the nature reserve, on the high plateaus of Vallo di Diano or through the Mingardo and Calore river valleys. Some farms in the interior that offer holiday accommodation also keep horses for their guests. *www.cilentohorseriding.com*, *www.agri urismoimoresani.com*

KAYAKING

When you tire of the sea and the beach and want to experience fresh, cool water in a wild, romantic mountainous landscape then a great option is to go kayaking through the Calore ravines and gorges near Felitto. The river valley is a natural oasis and is home to the Italian otter *(www.escursioninelcilento.135.it)*. Kayak and rafting trips are also available on the Sele or Tanagro rivers *(www.cam*

pobase.org, *www.tpescursioni.it)*. See the sea from another perspective: coastal kayak rides on the Amalfitana *(www. amalfikayak.com)*, in the Cilento *(www. italykayaktours.com)* and in Naples *(www.kayaknapoli.com)*.

PARAGLIDING

A top spot for hang-gliders and paragliders is only a short drive from the ancient temples of Paestum on the slopes of Monte Soprano. During the day a strong updraft develops with the south/south-westerly wind. A few minutes after take-off you can reach heights of 700 m/2300 ft. Starting and landing spots can be seen at *www.yumping.it*. The *Parapendio Le Streghe* club *(www.parapendiolestreghe. it)* offers courses and tourist flights in a two-seater.

SCUBA DIVING

Campania's coast and its islands are a diver's paradise and there are numerous dive schools in the resorts that supply dive equipment and offer course and dive trips. The foothills of the Sorrento Peninsula offers some great dive opportunities: the Punta Campanella's Parco Marino and the rocky cliffs of the Punta del Capo. In addition to the marine creatures and a rich underwater flora there is also Madonna dedicated to the seafarers in the diving grounds (at the Massa Lubrense harbour) and Christ's suffering depicted on 15 ceramic tiles (from Sorrento towards Punta del Capo). The INSIDER TIP underground grottos such as the Grotta dello Zaffiro at Punta Campanella, on the tip of the Sorrento Peninsula, are very impressive. A good address is *Diving Nettuno (Villaggio Nettuno | Marina del Cantone | tel. 08 18 08 10 51 | www.divingsorrento.*

com). You can dive everywhere along the Amalfi Coast; one dive centre follows the next.

The beautiful INSIDER TIP Cilento coastline is perforated by grottos and full of coves and bays making it ideal for divers, especially the rocky shores near Marina di Camerota, near Palinuro and the Capo Palinuro peninsula with the red coral reefs at the Capo Spartivento, the cliffs at Acciaroli and the Punta Licosa headland at Castellabate. In Palinuro, one of many dive addresses is *Palinuro Sub Diving Center | Via Porto | tel. 09 74 93 85 09 | www.palinurosub.it*

A very special experience is the diving in the underwater Archaeology Park of ● Baia near Naples: you dive INSIDER TIP between the remains of the once magnificent ancient Roman summer villas, e.g. with *Centro Sub Campi Flegrei (Via Napoli 1 | Pozzuoli | tel. 08 18 53 15 63 | www.centrosubcampiflegrei.it).*

WELLBEING

The spa and wellness industry is also expanding rapidly in Campania as elsewhere: an increasing number of the luxury hotels are now offering modern spa facilities while cosmetic salons and massage studios are opening up mainly in holiday resorts such as Positano or Capri and of course on Ischia with its splendid natural hot springs.

WINDSURFING & SAILING

Classic water sport activities such as sailing, stand-up paddling and surfing are offered all along the coast. Good surfing conditions can be found at Cetara, Paestum, Agropoli, Marina di Casal Velino and Palinuro.

The Campania is one of Italy's most attractive regions for divers

TRAVEL WITH KIDS

There are a lot of things that children (and adults) will find exciting on a holiday with such fascinating places as the bustling port of Naples, the winding and picturesque rocky coast of Amalfi, the mighty Mount Vesuvius volcano and the southern Cilento with its remote mountain landscape with forests, caves and divine sandy beaches.

How about a stroll across the *Campi Flegrei* (the "burning fields") of the Solfatara crater near Pozzuoli where stinky sulphur hisses and mud bubbles from holes in the ground? The view into the volcanic crater of *Mount Vesuvius (daily 9am–2 hrs before sunset | 10 euros, children 8 euros | www.guidevesuvio.it)* is also pretty exciting, especially a hike along the crater's edge, where steam still rises out of the lava vents.

It is best to drive to Naples with children on a Sunday: the seaside promenade, *Lungomare Caracciolo,* is closed to traffic from early morning until the afternoon and it is Neapolitan family time so young kids on their rollerblades can cruise along without any problems.

If your children are at an age when they are interested in (old) crafts, you should visit the museum of papermaking in Amalfi. They can also experience the old farming methods and crafts of Cilento – how to make olive oil, wool, shoes and hemp – in the small, thoughtfully done village museums, such as in *Moio della Civitella*, in *Montecorice*, in *Roscigno Vecchia* or in *Teggiano*.

Bubbling mud fields, the stinky smell of sulphur, vents spewing volcanic steam: Mount Vesuvius is way better than any amusement park

A trip down below the city into the underworld of Naples *(Napoli Sotteranea)* – with its fascinating caves, cellars, cisterns, tunnels – is guaranteed to make a big impression. And if your children like being spooked, then you should take them to the catacomb cemeteries where they can see real skeletons.

The Cilento coastline – with its crystal-clear water and wide, clean sandy beaches – is ideal for children while on the farmsteads in the hinterland *(agriturismo)* there are animals and family activi-ties. The hotels and holiday resorts on the coast all offer sports and in July and August (when the Italians come) a variety of children's activities and entertainment.

NAPLES

ACQUARIO E STAZIONE ZOOLOGICA ANTON DOHRN (U B5) (*ᗰ d6*)
There are about 30 pools full of different fish, sea creatures, algae and marine flora. The aquarium is nice and close to

A family workout in Pompeii – step aerobics for mum and leap frog for daughter

the sea in the tranquil, landscaped park of Villa Communale between the promenades Via Caracciolo and Riviera di Chiaia. *Nov–Feb Tue–Sun 9.30am–5pm, March–Oct Tue–Sun 9.30am–6.30pm | admission 1.50 euros, children (4–12 years) 1 euro | www.szn.it*

CRATERE DEGLI ASTRONI
(132 C5) (*Ø C4*)

The drive to Pozzuoli goes through stretches of countryside covered by an urban sprawl so you would never expect to find a natural paradise in an area like this. The nature reserve is north of the city motorway, and the smoking fields of Solfatara, and covers an area of just under 1 mile^2 of an extinct volcanic crater – an unspoilt landscape of maquis, chestnuts, holm oaks and a crater lake full of water

birds. Great to stroll around and just absorb the sights and sounds of nature. *Fri–Sun 9.30am–sunset | Tangenziale motorway, exit Agnano | www.wwf.it*

INSIDER TIP MAGIC WORLD
(132 B4) (*Ø B3*)

The large, modern amusement park near Licola (15 km/9 miles north-west of Naples) has various attractions such as (in summer) a water fun area with wave pool, swimming pools, water slides and rivers – the most elaborate facility in southern Italy. *June–mid Sept daily 10am–6pm, Fri–Sun until 10pm | admission 14 euros, Aug 18 euros, children up to 1.50 m 7 euros, Sat/Sun and Aug 10 euros, free for those up to 1 m, from 2pm reduced admission | www.magicworld.it*

INSIDER TIP MUSEO VIVO DI CITTÀ DELLA SCIENZA (132 C5) (*◻ C4*)

On the western outskirts of the city, on the way to Pozzuoli, there is this interesting, ultramodern science museum. The interactive exhibits detail how our world functions: how the cosmos works, how lightning is created and what our bodies look like inside. Also a section especially for small children. *Tue–Sat 9am–5pm, Sun 10am–7pm, shorter times in winter | admission 8 euros, children (3–17 years) 5.50 euros | Via Coroglio 104 | www.cittadellascienza.it*

OSPEDALE DELLE BAMBOLE
(U E2) (*◻ g3*)

This doll's paradise is a pure delight for small children: four generations of the Grassi family have been repairing dolls from around the world in their doll's hospital. *Mon–Sat 10.30am–3pm | Via San Biagio dei Librai 46 | www.ospedaledelle bambole.it*

HERCULANEUM & POMPEII

So that the visit to Pompeii with a pram (only off-road prams are suitable!) doesn't turn into a nightmare, the antiquities management (*www.pompeiisites.org*) recommends a shorter round trip from the entrance of Piazza Anfiteatro. Technology enthusiasts will enjoy a fascinating visit to the *Museo Archeologico Virtuale (March–May daily 9am–5.30pm, June–Sept 10am–6.30pm, Oct–Feb Tue–Sun 10am–4pm | 7.50 euros, children up to 18 years 6 euros | Via IV Novembre 44 | www. museomav.it)* in Ercolano.

CAPRI, ISCHIA, PROCIDA

ANTICA AENARIA (132 B6) (*◻ B5*)
Ischia is a paradise for children especially when you take them on a journey through time: 2000 years ago the sea level was several metres lower than it is today which is why part of an ancient Roman site now stands under water. Antica Aenaria is located at the foot of the castle at Ischia Ponte where archaeological findings from this underwater Roman settlement have been excavated. A cooperative organises tours in glass-bottom boats. *www.is chiabarche.it*

AMALFI COAST

PESCATURISMO (134 B–C5) (*◻ D–E6*)
Fishermen offer holidaymakers the opportunity to come along on their fishing trips, a tourist attraction known as **INSIDER TIP** *pescaturismo* which is available at Massa Lubrense *(Sima Pesca & Turismo | www.pescatouring.com)*, Vico Equense *(Cooperativa Pescatori San Francesco di Paola)*, Sorrento *(Cooperativa Ulixes on the beach Marina della Lobra)* and Cilento. Ask for *pescaturismo* directly at the ports or in tourist information offices..

PAESTUM & CILENTO NATIONAL PARK

EXCURSION BOAT WITH PICNIC
(138–139 C–D6) (*◻ L–M 11–12*)

In the summer months along the Cilento coast fishermen ferry holidaymakers (especially from Marina di Camerota and Palinuro) to the bays and coves with their bizarre rock formations and wonderful sea caves. The trips often include a picnic on the beach, where the fishermen grill fresh fish. A special experience for both children and adults: night tours under the stars. The boat trips can also be combined with coastal walks. *Information and bookings at the harbours*

FESTIVALS & EVENTS

Botti, botti, sempre botti – firecrackers, firecrackers, always firecrackers – is the Neapolitan motto, no matter what the occasion is: be it Christmas, New Year, patron saint festivals or a Napoli football team win, even improvised street markets are celebrated with fireworks and rockets

FESTIVALS & EVENTS

EASTER

In the *settimana santa* there are often **processions** that move through the streets, the most impressive ones on Good Friday in Procida and in Sorrento. On Easter Monday families picnic outdoors. On Easter Monday the INSIDER TIP *Madonna dell'Arco* is celebrated in the church of pilgrimage Sant' (impressive INSIDER TIP collection of votive pictures, a chronicle of misfortunes, from pirate raids in the 16th century to today's drug addiction) near Pomigliano d'Arco at the foot of Mount Vesuvius with *Lunedì in Albis,* and crowds of white-clad, ecstatically pious, barefoot *fujenti.*

APRIL/MAY

On the Saturday before the first Sunday in May, Neapolitan worshippers gather in the cathedral to witness the liquefying of blood of their saint, **San Gennaro.**

MAY

Maggio dei Monumenti: on the weekends villas, monasteries, palaces, churches, and gardens in Naples are open for cultural events.

At the end of May the *Regata dei Tre Golfi* sailing regatta takes place in Capri for a week.

The *Wine in the City* festival in Naples offers over 100 wine-tasting opportunities in stores, museums, private homes and other unusual locations.

JUNE

⭐ *I Gigli* in Nola near Naples: eight large, colourful towers dance through the alleys on the shoulders of members of the old craft guilds on the Sunday after the 22 June.

On the 24th ⭐ *San Giovanni Battista* (John the Baptist) is celebrated in Buonopane on Ischia. The evening starts with the symbolic sword dance *'ndrezzata.*

The ambitious avant-garde festival ⭐ ● *Napoli Teatro Festival Italia* showcases some of the most interesting sites in the city and the Gulf.

Loud, colourful and lively: religious fervour and noisy enthusiasm characterise the festival calendar around the Gulf of Naples

On 27 June Amalfi celebrates its patron at sea and on land at the *Festa di Sant'Andrea.*

JUNE, JULY, SEPTEMBER
Festival Musicale di Ravello: the setting inspired Wagner, rich and varied programme

AUGUST
Ferragosto, the highlight of the Italian summer on 15 Aug, is celebrated everywhere by everyone
La Notte del Mito: a fantastic party with mythological fancy dress at the end of August in the Il Ciclope grotto disco in Marina di Camerota

AUGUST/SEPTEMBER
Pomigliano Jazz: famous jazz festival in Pomigliano d'Arco, a municipality of Naples

SEPTEMBER
Food harvest festivals throughout the month of September (wine, chestnuts etc.).

Leuciana Festival: Theatre, ballet and concert performances in Capua, Caserta and San Leucio, the Bourbon town of silk

NATIONAL HOLIDAYS

1 Jan	*Capodanno* (New Year)
6 Jan	*Epifania* (Epiphany)
March/April	*Pasquetta* (Easter Monday)
25 April	*Liberazione* (Lieberation from fascism)
1 May	*Festa del Lavoro* (Labour Day)
2 June	*Festa della Repubblica* (Republic Day)
15 Aug	*Ferragosto* (Assumption)
1 Nov	*Ognissanti* (All Saint's Day)
8 Dec	*Immacolata Concezione* (Immaculate Conception)
25 Dec	*Natale* (Christmas)
26 Dec	*Santo Stefano* (Boxing Day)

LINKS, BLOGS, APPS & MORE

LINKS & BLOGS

www.italyguides.it/us/napoli/naples.htm A virtual journey, with dozens of 360° panorama views, takes you to the most famous sites in the city. Furthermore, you can enjoy these in free HD videos, download audio guides and make hotel reservations

www.campaniameteo.it Weather forecast for every part of the region. The many webcams help to overcome the language barrier

www.capware.it Virtual reconstructions of the buried cities around Vesuvius of AD 79

www.in-campania.it Official cultural and tourism site of the region of Campania with an events calendar

www.inaples.it The city of Naples portal has museum info, accommodation and the monthly booklet 'Qui Napoli' pro- gramme (also with tips about events) as a free download

www.naplesgreeters.it Naples seen from a Neapolitan perspective: Let a local show you around the city free of charge. Greeters are voluntary guides who want to share their enthusiasm and love for their city with visitors by taking them on their own personal tour of Naples

www.portanapoli.com Private site full of practical tips and background information about Naples and Campania

www.napoliunplugged.com/ Bonnie Alberts, journalist and photographer, blogs from her adopted home of Naples; included are sections on the nightlife, shopping and information about upcoming events

www.ciaoamalfi.com A good website to explore for travel tips and inspira- tion, this blog is written by an expat

writer and art historian, with entertaining snippets about daily life on Italy's Amalfi Coast

www.capri.net/en/e/capri-e-il-cinema# Article about movies shot on Capri – Sophia Loren and Brigitte Bardot get you into the right mood

www.youtube.com/watch?v=PlZ-SGfp6Os exciting BBC documentation in English on "the last day in Pompeii"

VIDEOS & MUSIC

www.youtube.com/watch?v=ybnxOud2IGM What appears at first glance to show the traffic chaos in Naples's Quartieri Spagnoli, this video is in fact testimony to the success of the shared space traffic concept

www.youtube.com/watch?v=1bsmv6PyKs0&feature=youtu.be Black and white film footage of the 1944 eruption of Mount Vesuvius

www.radionaples.com RadioNaples broadcasts *musica napoletana* round the clock, player for Windows and Apple

www.youtube.com/watch?v=OXDByxV-k5s Nostalgic black and white footage from 1955 of the Amalfi coast

Babbel – Italian for an iPhone: easy, snappy way to learn Italian

● Radio Partenope Web Radio plays Neapolitan music from classic to pop

Pompei Map and Walks Pompeii guide on the go, additional content costs extra

Napoli Teatro Festival Italia A practical guide to the shows, the locations and the events of the famous theatre festival

APPS

TRAVEL TIPS

ACCOMMODATION

Private hosts are an alternative to hotels: *www.airbnb.com, www.wimdu.com* or *www.9flats.com*. The tourist site of the Regione Campania – *www.incampania.com* – has directories of every kind of accommodation. Information about B&B addresses: *www.bb-napoli.com, www.rentabed.it* or *www.bedandbreakfast.it.* A favourite is also agriturismo: *www.aiab.it/agriturismi, www.agriturist.com, www.bioagriturismi.it, www.soloagriturismo.com.*

ARRIVAL

✈ A number of airlines fly from the UK directly to Naples airport Capodichino *(www.portal.gesac.it)*. These include British Airways *(www.britishairways.com)*, Alitalia *(www.alitalia.com)*, Ryanair *(www.ryanair.com)* and easyJet *(www.easyjet.com)*. If you're flying from North America, you will likely have a stopover in a major city such as London, Paris or Rome. The airport bus Alibus runs every 15 minutes to the city centre (Piazza Garibaldi and, directly at the port Molo Beverello, Piazza Municipio). A shuttle bus at Beverello port takes you onwards to the ferry port Calata Porta di Massa. There are also bus connections to Sorrento.

🚗 There is little advantage to arriving in Naples and the islands with your own car (there are car rentals in Naples, Sorrento, Salerno) as traffic congestion and parking are a very real problem. However, a car is more practical in Paestum and the Cilento. The motorway runs from the Brenner pass via Bologna, Rome, Caserta and Salerno. It is 1100 km/683 miles from the Brenner to Palinuro.

🚆 Travelling by train from the UK involves several changes in Italy, either in Milan or Rome. Naples has three railway stations, Centrale, Mergellina and Campi Flegrei (Fuorigrotta). There are hourly connections to Rome and Salerno and trains from Naples and Salerno to the Cilento coast. The Circumvesuviana railway runs from the main station every half hour via Pompeii to Sorrento. On the station forecourt, Piazza Garibaldi, intercity buses leave for Caserta, Amalfi and Salerno. A taxi to the hotels in the city costs about 10 euros.

RESPONSIBLE TRAVEL

It doesn't take a lot to be environmentally friendly whilst travelling. Don't just think about your carbon footprint whilst flying to and from your holiday destination but also about how you can protect nature and culture abroad. As a tourist it is especially important to respect nature, look out for local products, cycle instead of driving, save water and much more. If you would like to find out more about eco-tourism please visit: *www.ecotourism.org*

CAR HIRE

Online offers are available from about 30 euros per day. On weekends a mid size vehicle costs 130–160 euros or 300–500 euros per week. Reservations prior to departure are often cheaper. Rental cars in Cilento: *www.antares91.com*

From arrival to weather

Holiday from start to finish: the most important addresses and information for your Campania trip

CITY TOURS

On board double-decker buses, tourists can take two tours of the city: line A (60 min.) takes you through the city centre while line B (70 min.) cruises ● along the coast to Mergellina and Posillipo. Combined ticket *22 euros | www.napoli.city-sightseeing.it*

CONSULATES & EMBASSIES

BRITISH EMBASSY
Via Venti Settembre, 80/a | 00187 Rome | tel. +39 06 42 20 00 01 | www.ukinitaly.fco.gov.uk

UNITED STATES CONSULATE
Piazza della Repubblica | 80122 Naples | tel. +39 08 15 83 81 11 | naples.usconsulate.gov

CUSTOMS

EU citizens can import and export goods for their personal use tax-free (800 cigarettes, 1 kg tobacco, 90L of wine, 10L of spirits over 22% vol.). Visitors from other countries must observe the following limits. Duty free are: max. 50g perfume, 200 cigarettes, 50 cigars, 250g tobacco, 1L of spirits (over 22% vol.), 2L of spirits (under 22% vol.), 2L of any wine.

DRIVING

The maximum speed in built-up areas is 50 km/h (30 mph), on main roads 90 km/h (55 mph), on dual carriageways 110 km/h (66 mph), and 130 km/h (80 mph) on motorways (110 km/h/66 mph in rain; 50 km/h/30 mph in fog). It is mandatory to drive with dipped headlights outside built-up areas during the day. Italy has stricter drink driving laws than the UK, only allowing 0.5 per mil. It is compulsory to carry visibility vests in the car. Most highways have a toll fee. Filling stations are generally open Mon–Sat 7.30am–12.30pm and 3pm–7pm, a few garages open on Sundays, always along motorways. Otherwise the automatic fuel dispensers help. A breakdown service by the ACI for a fee: *tel 80 31 16, www.aci.it; mobile tel. 8 00 11 68 00.*

EMERGENCY SERVICES

Toll free EU emergency number: *tel. 112* (police, fire, ambulance).

CURRENCY CONVERTER

£	€	€	£
1	1.17	1	0.85
3	3.50	3	2.56
5	5.86	5	4.26
13	15.24	13	11.09
40	47	40	34.11
75	88	75	63.96
120	141	120	102
250	293	250	213
500	586	500	426

$	€	€	$
1	0.94	1	1.06
3	2.82	3	3.19
5	4.70	5	5.32
13	12.22	13	13.83
40	37.60	40	42.55
75	70.50	75	79.78
120	113	120	128
250	235	250	266
500	470	500	532

For current exchange rates see www.xe.com

...puccino	£0.80–1.20/$1.50–1.90 *for a cup at the counter*
...etrol	£1.20/$1.50 *for 1 L of super*
Wine	From £2/$3.20 *for a glass of wine*
Snack	From £2/$3.20 *for a panino*
Beach	£8–16/$13–26 per day *for two sun loungers and umbrella*
Bus ride	£0.80/$1.50 *for a bus or Metro ride in Naples*

ENTRANCE FEES

Most museums and historic/excavation sites cost about 6 euros, Pompeii and Ercolano cost 13/11 euros. Many discounts are available with the *Campania Arte Card (www.campaniartecard.it)*, a tourist pass for 3 or 7 days' duration, which you can use for almost all museums and excavation sites in Naples and the region of Campania for free or at reduced prices, depending on the combination (from 21 euros, under 25 years from 12 euros), and it includes public transport and heritage site buses. You can buy it at tourist offices, at train stations and at airports, in museums and in many hotels. EU citizens under 18 years receive free entrance into government museums and excavation sites (18–25 years 50% discount, with ID). Additionally, admission is free in state (and some private) museums on the first Sunday every month.

FERRIES

Naples has two harbours: hydrofoils *(aliscafo)* and fast boats to the islands and to Sorrento dock at *Molo Beverello (Stazione Marittima)*, car ferries *(traghetto)* at the *Calata Porta di Massa* north of Molo Angioino. The *aliscafi* to Ischia and Procida leave from Mergellina harbour. There are car ferries from Pozzuoli to Procida and Ischia. The ferry connections between Sorrento and Capri are also good. From Salerno there are ferries going to Amalfi and Capri in summer, from Naples and Capri to Positano and Amalfi. From April to September there are fast boats to Cilento. *www.aliscafi.it, www.navlib.it, www. traghettilines.it, www.capritourism.com*

INFORMATION

ITALIAN STATE TOURISM BOARD (ENIT)
– *1 Princes St. | London W1B 2AY |tel. 020 74 08 12 54 | www.italiantouristboard.co.uk*
– *686 Park Avenue | New York, NY 10065 | tel. 212 245 56 18 | www.italiantourism.com*

MONEY & CREDIT CARDS

Almost all banks have ATMs *(bancomat)*; many restaurants, hotels and shops, toll stations and filling stations accept credit cards.

OPENING HOURS

Grocery stores are generally open Mon–Sat 8.30am–1pm and 5.30pm–8pm, boutiques and supermarkets 8.30am or 9am–12.30pm and 4pm–7.30pm. In coastal towns the shops often stay open later. Churches are usually closed from 12.30pm to 5pm. The last admission to places of interest is usually one hour before closing. The times of most churches and places of interest can now be found online.

PHONE & MOBILE PHONE

Phoning via fixed network is only possible from very few public phone boxes and bars. Telephone cards can be purchased in tobacconists. If you make many phone calls, you can purchase an Italian SIM card (3, TIM, Vodafone, Wind). The country code for Italy is *0039*, for the UK *0044*, for the US *001*. It is necessary to dial the *0* at the beginning of each fixed-line connection – both from abroad and when making local calls.

PUBLIC TRANSPORT

In Naples there is a good bus network, two underground lines and four cable cars. Tickets for city buses are available at tobacconists and at newspaper kiosks. There are intercity buses and/or regular train connections to all the important places in Campania. Good connections with local trains to Pozzuoli, Baia, Cuma,

Ercolano, Pompeii, Sorrento. Public tr... port is relatively cheap. In the summ... Cilentobus runs from Naples to Cilento *www.muoversincampania.it, www.orar-iautobus.it, www.agenziainfanteviaggi.it/cilento-bus.html*

WEATHER, WHEN TO GO

High season: mid July to end of August, with a peak around 15 August: the prices for accommodation double or triple during this time; driving somewhere or finding a parking space on the Amalfi Coast is practically impossible. The best time to travel: May, June, Sept, from Nov to Easter it can be difficult finding open hotels, especially in the Cilento. The Amalfi Coast is also very busy during Christmas and New Year.

WEATHER IN NAPLES

	Jan	Feb	March	April	May	June	July	Aug	Sept	Oct	Nov	Dec
Daytime temperatures in °C/°F	11/52	12/54	15/59	18/64	22/72	27/81	29/84	29/84	26/79	21/70	17/63	13/55
Nighttime temperatures in °C/°F	6/43	6/43	8/46	11/52	14/57	18/64	20/68	20/68	18/64	14/57	11/52	7/45
☀	4	4	5	7	8	10	11	10	7	6	5	5
☂	10	9	8	7	6	4	2	3	6	9	11	12
≈	14/57	13/55	14/57	15/59	18/64	21/70	24/75	25/77	23/73	21/70	18/64	16/61

☀ Sunshine hours/day ☂ Precipitation days/month ≈ Water temperature in °C/°F

USEFUL PHRASES
ITALIAN

PRONUNCIATION

c, cc	before e or i like ch in "church", e.g. ciabatta, otherwise like k
ch, cch	like k, e.g. pacchi, che
g, gg	before e or i like j in "just", e.g. gente, otherwise like g in "get"
gl	like "lli" in "million", e.g. figlio
gn	as in "cognac", e.g. bagno
sc	before e or i like sh, e.g. uscita
sch	like sk in "skill", e.g. Ischia
z	at the beginning of a word like dz in "adze", otherwise like ts

An accent on an Italian word shows that the stress is on the last syllable.
In other cases we have shown which syllable is stressed by placing a dot below the relevant vowel.

IN BRIEF

Yes/No/Maybe	Sì/No/Forse
Please/Thank you	Per favore/Grazie
Excuse me, please!	Scusa!/Mi scusi
May I...?/Pardon?	Posso...? / Come dice?/Prego?
I would like to.../Have you got...?	Vorrei.../Avete ...?
How much is...?	Quanto costa...?
I (don't) like that	(Non) mi piace
good/bad	buono/cattivo/bene/male
broken/doesn't work	guasto/non funziona
too much/much/little/all/nothing	troppo/molto/poco/ tutto/niente
Help!/Attention!/Caution!	aiuto!/attenzione!/prudenza!
ambulance/police/fire brigade	ambulanza/polizia/vigili del fuoco
Prohibition/forbidden/danger/dangerous	divieto/vietato/pericolo/pericoloso
May I take a photo here/of you?	Posso fotografar La?

GREETINGS, FAREWELL

Good morning!/afternoon!/evening!/night!	Buon giorno!/Buon giorno!/Buona sera!/Buona notte!
Hello! / Goodbye!/See you	Ciao!/Salve! / Arrivederci!/Ciao!
My name is...	Mi chiamo...
What's your name?	Come si chiama?/Come ti chiami
I'm from...	Vengo da...

Parli italiano?

"Do you speak Italian?" This guide will help you to say the bas words and phrases in Italian

DATE & TIME

Monday/Tuesday/Wednesday	lunedì/martedì/mercoledì
Thursday/Friday/Saturday	giovedì/venerdì/sabato
Sunday/holiday/ working day	domenica/(giorno) festivo/ (giorno) feriale
today/tomorrow/yesterday	oggi/domani/ieri
hour/minute	ora/minuto
day/night/week/month/year	giorno/notte/settimana/mese/anno
What time is it?	Che ora è? Che ore sono?
It's three o'clock/It's half past three	Sono le tre/Sono le tre e mezza
a quarter to four	le quattro meno un quarto/ un quarto alle quattro

TRAVEL

open/closed	aperto/chiuso
entrance/exit	entrata/uscita
departure/arrival	partenza/arrivo
toilets/ladies/gentlemen	bagno/toilette/signore/signori
(no) drinking water	acqua (non) potabile
Where is...?/Where are...?	Dov'è...?/Dove sono...?
left/right/straight ahead/back	sinistra/destra/dritto/indietro
close/far	vicino/lontano
bus/tram	bus/tram
taxi/cab	taxi/tassì
bus stop/cab stand	fermata/posteggio taxi
parking lot/parking garage	parcheggio/parcheggio coperto
street map/map	pianta/mappa
train station/harbour	stazione/porto
airport	aeroporto
schedule/ticket	orario/biglietto
supplement	supplemento
single/return	solo andata/andata e ritorno
train/track	treno/binario
platform	banchina/binario
I would like to rent...	Vorrei noleggiare...
a car/a bicycle	una macchina/una bicicletta
a boat	una barca
petrol/gas station	distributore/stazione di servizio
petrol/gas / diesel	benzina/diesel/gasolio
breakdown/repair shop	guasto/officina

...ld you please book a table for night for four?	Vorrei prenotare per stasera un tavolo per quattro?
on the terrace/by the window	sulla terrazza/ vicino alla finestra
The menu, please	La carta/il menù, per favore
Could I please have...?	Potrei avere...?
bottle/carafe/glass	bottiglia/caraffa/bicchiere
knife/fork/spoon/salt/pepper	coltello/forchetta/cucchiaio/sale/pepe
sugar/vinegar/oil/milk/cream/lemon	zucchero/aceto/olio/latte/panna/limone
cold/too salty/not cooked	freddo/troppo salato/non cotto
with/without ice/sparkling	con/senza ghiaccio/gas
vegetarian/allergy	vegetariano/vegetariana/allergia
May I have the bill, please?	Vorrei pagare/Il conto, per favore
bill/tip	conto/mancia

SHOPPING

Where can I find...?	Dove posso trovare...?
I'd like.../I'm looking for ...	Vorrei.../Cerco...
Do you put photos onto CD?	Vorrei masterizzare delle foto su CD?
pharmacy/shopping centre/kiosk	farmacia/centro commerciale/edicola
department store/supermarket	grandemagazzino/supermercato
baker/market/grocery	forno/ mercato/negozio alimentare
photographic items/newspaper shop/	articoli per foto/giornalaio
100 grammes/1 kilo	un etto/un chilo
expensive/cheap/price/more/less	caro/economico/prezzo/di più/di meno
organically grown	di agricoltura biologica

ACCOMMODATION

I have booked a room	Ho prenotato una camera
Do you have any... left?	Avete ancora...
single room/double room	una (camera) singola/doppia
breakfast/half board/	prima colazione/mezza pensione/
full board (American plan)	pensione completa
at the front/seafront/lakefront	con vista/con vista sul mare/lago
shower/sit-down bath/balcony/terrace	doccia/bagno/balcone/terrazza
key/room card	chiave/scheda magnetica
luggage/suitcase/bag	bagaglio/valigia/borsa

BANKS, MONEY & CREDIT CARDS

bank/ATM/pin code	banca/bancomat/ codice segreto
cash/credit card	in contanti/carta di credito
bill/coin/change	banconota/moneta/il resto

HEALTH

doctor/dentist/paediatrician	medico/dentista/pediatra
hospital/emergency clinic	ospedale/pronto soccorso/guardia medica
fever/pain/inflamed/injured	febbre/dolori/infiammato/ferito
diarrhoea/nausea/sunburn	diarrea/nausea/scottatura solare
plaster/bandage/ointment/cream	cerotto/fasciatura/pomata/crema
pain reliever/tablet/suppository	antidolorifico/compressa/supposta

POST, TELECOMMUNICATIONS & MEDIA

stamp/letter/postcard	francobollo/lettera/cartolina
I need a landline phone card/	Mi serve una scheda telefonica per la
I'm looking for a prepaid card for my	rete fissa/Cerco una scheda prepagata
mobile	per il mio cellulare
Where can I find internet access?	Dove trovo un accesso internet?
dial/connection/engaged	comporre/linea/occupato
socket/adapter/charger	presa/riduttore/caricabatterie
computer/battery/rechargeable battery	computer/batteria/accumulatore
internet address (URL)/e-mail address	indirizzo internet/indirizzo email
internet connection/wifi	collegamento internet/wi-fi
e-mail/file/print	email/file/stampare

LEISURE, SPORTS & BEACH

beach/bathing beach	spiaggia/bagno/stabilimento balneare
sunshade/lounger/cable car/chair lift	ombrellone/sdraio/funivia/seggiovia
(rescue) hut/avalanche	rifugio/valanga

NUMBERS

0	zero	15	quindici
1	uno	16	sedici
2	due	17	diciassette
3	tre	18	diciotto
4	quattro	19	diciannove
5	cinque	20	venti
6	sei	21	ventuno
7	sette	50	cinquanta
8	otto	100	cento
9	nove	200	duecento
10	dieci	1000	mille
11	undici	2000	duemila
12	dodici	10000	diecimila
13	tredici	½	un mezzo
14	quattordici	¼	un quarto

ROAD ATLAS

██ The green line indicates the Discovery Tour
"Naples & the Amalfi Coast at a glance"
██ The blue line indicates the other Discovery Tours

All tours are also marked on the pull-out map

Photo: Castello Aragonese, Ischia

Exploring Naples & the Amalfi Coast

The map on the back cover shows how the area has been sub-divided

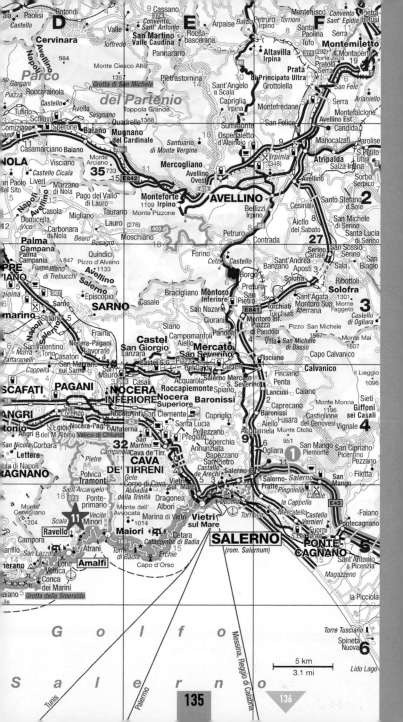

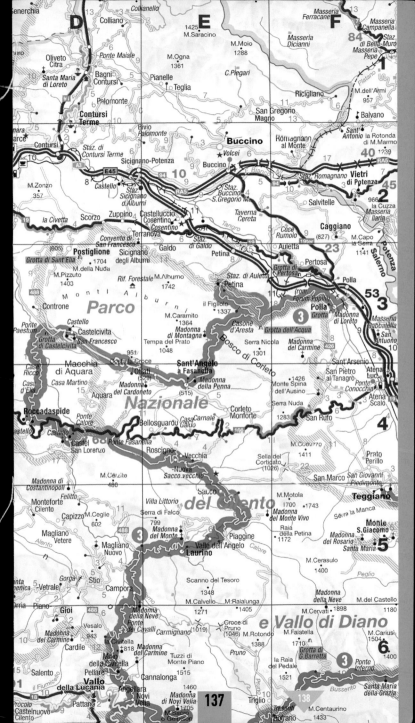

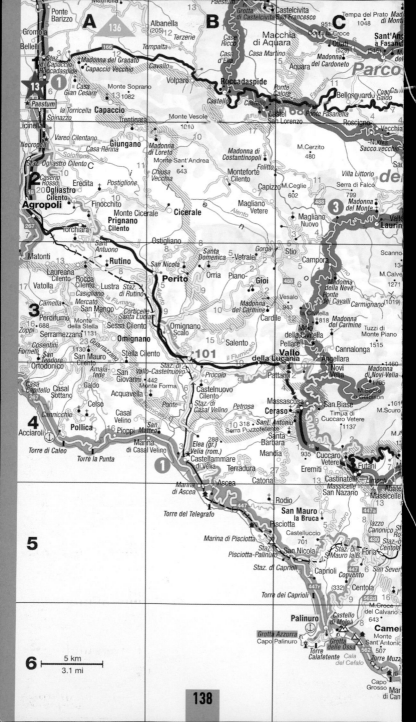

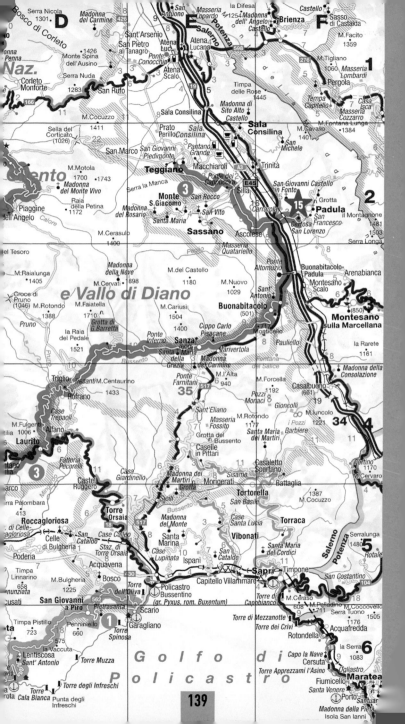

KEY TO ROAD ATLAS

German	Symbol	English
Autobahn mit Anschlussstelle und Anschlussnummern	Viernheim	Motorway with junction and junction number
Autobahn in Bau mit voraussichtlichem Fertigstellungsdatum	Datum · Date	Motorway under construction with expected date of opening
Rasthaus mit Übernachtung · Raststätte	Kassel	Hotel, motel · Restaurant
Kiosk · Tankstelle		Snackbar · Filling-station
Autohof · Parkplatz mit WC	P	Truckstop · Parking place with WC
Autobahn-Gebührenstelle		Toll station
Autobahnähnliche Schnellstraße		Dual carriageway with motorway characteristics
Fernverkehrsstraße		Trunk road
Verbindungsstraße		Main road
Nebenstraßen		Secondary roads
Fahrweg · Fußweg		Carriageway · Footpath
Gebührenpflichtige Straße		Toll road
Straße für Kraftfahrzeuge gesperrt	X X X X X X	Road closed for motor vehicles
Straße für Wohnanhänger gesperrt		Road closed for caravans
Straße für Wohnanhänger nicht empfehlenswert		Road not recommended for caravans
Autofähre · Autozug-Terminal		Car ferry · Autorail station
Hauptbahn · Bahnhof · Tunnel		Main line railway · Station · Tunnel
Besonders sehenswertes kulturelles Objekt	♪ Neuschwanstein	Cultural site of particular interest
Besonders sehenswertes landschaftliches Objekt	✳ Breitachklamm	Landscape of particular interest
MARCO POLO Erlebnistour 1		MARCO POLO Discovery Tour 1
MARCO POLO Erlebnistouren		MARCO POLO Discovery Tours
MARCO POLO Highlight	★	MARCO POLO Highlight
Landschaftlich schöne Strecke		Route with beautiful scenery
Touristenstraße	Hanse-Route	Tourist route
Museumseisenbahn		Tourist train
Kirche, Kapelle · Kirchenruine Kloster · Klosterruine		Church, chapel · Church ruin Monastery · Monastery ruin
Schloss, Burg · Burgruine Turm · Funk-, Fernsehturm		Palace, castle · Castle ruin Tower · Radio or TV tower
Leuchtturm · Windmühle Denkmal · Soldatenfriedhof		Lighthouse · Windmill Monument · Military cemetery
Ruine, frühgeschichtliche Stätte · Höhle Hotel, Gasthaus, Berghütte · Heilbad		Archaeological excavation, ruins · Cave Hotel, inn, refuge · Spa
Campingplatz · Jugendherberge Schwimmbad, Erlebnisbad, Strandbad · Golfplatz		Camping site · Youth hostel Swimming pool, leisure pool, beach · Golf-course
Botanischer Garten, sehenswerter Park · Zoologischer Garten		Botanical gardens, interesting park · Zoological garden
Bedeutendes Bauwerk · Bedeutendes Areal		Important building · Important area
Verkehrsflughafen · Regionalflughafen	✈ ⊕	Airport · Regional airport
Flugplatz · Segelflugplatz	⊕	Airfield · Gliding site
Boots- und Jachthafen		Marina

FOR YOUR NEXT TRIP...

MARCO POLO TRAVEL GUIDES

Algarve
Amsterdam
Andalucia
Athens
Australia
Austria
Bali & Lombok
Bangkok
Barcelona
Berlin
Brazil
Bruges
Brussels
Budapest
Bulgaria
California
Cambodia
Canada East
Canada West / Rockies
& Vancouver
Cape Town &
Garden Route
Cape Verde
Channel Islands
Chicago & The Lakes
China
Cologne
Copenhagen
Corfu
Costa Blanca
& Valencia
Costa Brava
Costa del Sol
& Granada
Crete
Cuba
Cyprus
(North and South)
Dresden

Dubai
Dublin
Dubrovnik &
Dalmatian Coast
Edinburgh
Egypt
Egypt Red Sea Resorts
Finland
Florence
Florida
French Atlantic Coast
French Riviera
(Nice, Cannes &
Monaco)
Fuerteventura
Gran Canaria
Greece
Hamburg
Hong Kong & Macau
Iceland
India
India South
Ireland
Israel
Istanbul
Italy
Jordan
Kos
Krakow
Lake Garda
Lanzarote
Las Vegas
Lisbon
London
Los Angeles
Madeira & Porto Santo
Madrid
Mallorca
Malta & Gozo

Mauritius
Menorca
Milan
Montenegro
Morocco
Munich
Naples & Amalfi Coast
New York
New Zealand
Norway
Oslo
Paris
Phuket
Portugal
Prague
Rhodes
Rome
San Francisco
Sardinia
Scotland
Seychelles
Shanghai
Sicily
Singapore
South Africa
Sri Lanka
Stockholm
Switzerland
Tenerife
Thailand
Turkey
Turkey South Coast
Tuscany
United Arab Emirates
USA Southwest
(Las Vegas, Colorado,
New Mexico, Arizona
& Utah)
Venice
Vienna
Vietnam
Zakynthos & Ithaca,
Kefalonia, Lefkas

The travel guides with
Insider
Tips

INDEX

This index lists all places and destinations featured in this guide. Numbers in bold indicate a main entry.